BELONG TO THE WORLD
BRING YOUR TRIBE

PRAISE FOR

BELONG TO THE WORLD BRING YOUR TRIBE

"BELONG TO THE WORLD BRING YOUR TRIBE is Lauren Zinn's vision of a Jewish future that is nondual, universal, integral, inclusive, detached from political Zionism, aligned with liberal democracy, and open to learning alongside and from other religions. It is a roadmap for the evolution of all religions that should be read as a catalyst for the transformation of your religion."

- RABBI RAMI SHAPIRO, *Award-winning author, Adjunct Professor of Religion at Middle Tennessee State University, Co-Founder of the Snowmass Group, One River Foundation and Big I Conference on Inclusive Theology, Spirituality, and Consciousness*

"The topic for this book could not be more urgent and the title more apt. Zinn has spoken to our moment in history. We must hold our tribes with ever more love and care, even as we show up for each other in these perilous times. Zinn leads the way."

- RABBI NANCY FUCHS KREIMER, Ph.D. *Founding Director, Multifaith* Studies *and Initiative, Reconstructionist Rabbinical College, Emerita*

"For anyone worried about the future of our war-torn, conflict-ridden, seemingly broken world, Lauren Zinn's book offers a vista of hope. *BELONG TO THE WORLD BRING YOUR TRIBE* is a work of rare courage, wisdom, and candor. It points beyond fear and tribalism to a shared life animated by deep listening and mutual care."

- JULIAN LEVINSON, Ph.D. *Samuel Shetzer Professor of American Jewish Studies and Professor of English at the University of Michigan. Author, Exiles on Main Street: Jewish American Writers and American Literary Culture*

"Groundbreaking!! *BELONG TO THE WORLD BRING YOUR TRIBE* is an amazing tour de force! It is a combination of mind-expanding creativity and scholarly documentation focused on the evolution of interfaith and interspiritual possibilities for the Jewish community and larger world. Using personal experience and clear vision, Zinn brings antagonistic forces into a new synthesis. May this vision lead us forward into the next turn of the wheel."

- LUCINDA KURTZ, M.A., *Jewish Renewal Sage-ing Mentor, Ritualist, Poet, and Brennan Healing Science Practitioner*

"*BELONG TO THE WORLD BRING YOUR TRIBE: A New Vision for Judaism* offers a compelling vision in these challenging times. Lauren Zinn is an intellectual force advancing the new Judaism."

- BARRY CHECKOWAY, Ph.D., *Arthur Dunham Collegiate Professor* Emeritus *of Social Work, School of Social Work, and Professor Emeritus of Urban Planning, Taubman College of Architecture and Urban Planning at the University of Michigan*

"I could not be more impressed or moved by what Lauren Zinn has accomplished in BELONG TO THE WORLD BRING YOUR TRIBE. It's a masterpiece - a brilliant, personal, passionate and very learned plea for, and exploration of, how we human beings (Jewish or otherwise) can vastly improve our relationship to and with the world and each other."

- SIMONE YEHUDA, Screenwriter, Playwright, Poet

"Religion - is that still a thing?' In BELONG TO THE WORLD BRING YOUR TRIBE, Zinn bravely answers Yes, but, if it and all of us are going to survive, religion must change. It must move to 'a new good heart,' open to our religious family but also to other religious families. Zinn reinforces the notion that interspirituality is not a blend of all religions but a way to practice your own in relationship with others practicing theirs. Zinn is right; religion lived this new way could help all religions (and us) survive - and thrive."

- JEANINE DILLER, Ph.D., *Associate Professor, Philosophy and Religious Studies, Judith Herb College of Arts, Social Sciences and Education, and Religious Studies Advisor, The University of Toledo*

"Lauren Zinn has written an important addition to the scant literature on the interfaith and interspiritual world into which we are all heading. Her perspective as an interfaith educator brings essential new stories, context, and wisdom to the experience of spiritual complexity, diversity, and abundance."

- SUSAN KATZ MILLER, *Journalist and Author, Being Both: Embracing Two Religions in One Interfaith Family and The Interfaith Family Workbook*

BELONG TO THE WORLD BRING YOUR TRIBE

A New Vision for Judaism

Lauren Zinn, Ph.D., Rev.

Copyright © 2026 Lauren I. Zinn
All Rights Reserved.

No part of this publication may be reproduced, distributed, or transmitted in any form or by any means or stored in a database or retrieval system, without the prior written permission of the copyright holder except for the use of brief quotations in a book review. All inquiries should be directed to zinnhouse.com

ISBN: 979-8-9930945-0-2 (paperback)
ISBN: 979-8-9930945-1-9 (eBook)
Library of Congress Control Number: 2025919372

Text Copyright © 2010-2026 Lauren I. Zinn
Original Art Copyright © 2008-2026 Lauren I. Zinn
ZinnHouse "Z" Logo by David Zinn
Cover Design by Kate Peterson
Technical Assistance by Kate Peterson

ZinnHouse
Printed in USA

DEDICATION

To all my family
with love.

OF BLESSED MEMORY

z'l

Zichronoh/ah/et l'vrocha

Mitch Rycus

Howard Adelman

Rabbi Burt Jacobson

Georgia Olson

Rabbi Joseph H. Gelberman

Gerald W. Isenberg

Steven M. Isenberg

I did not know Samantha Woll, a Jewish community leader and interfaith advocate, whose legacy is an inspiration.

CONTENTS

FOREWORD *by Barry Checkoway*

INTRODUCTION *Interspiritual Judaism: A Vision*   1

PART ONE

BELONG TO THE WORLD   17

    1 Getting Unstuck   23

    2 Integral and Interspiritual   29

    3 Evolutionary and Nondual   37

    4 Multiple Belonging   41

    5 If You Meet a Religious Leader on the Road   45

    6 How Does Europe Do It?   51

    7 Global Citizens Do It   53

    8 Growing *with* God   59

    9 A New-Fangled Preacher Teacher   65

    10 Tips for Belonging   69

PART TWO

BRING YOUR TRIBE   77

    1 Judaism's Gift: Exile and Return   87

    2 Jewish Identity, Again   91

    3 Roadmap to No Other Land   95

    4 Modern Israel?   99

    5 Reparations: Spiritual Activism   105

    6 Loving Ducks   113

    7 Can Barbie Save Israel? PS And the US?   117

    8 Rabbis in a Bar   123

9 Leaders, Teachers, Healers	127
10 Post-Tribal Judaism, Interspiritual Humanity	133

PART THREE
BECOME INTERSPIRITUALLY JEWISH — *137*

1 Hanukkah and Hegel	145
2 Interspiritual Hanukkah	149
3 Being Jewish in America In December	155
4 Purim Plus	159
5 Passover's Process	163
6 Ten Plagues of Money	165
7 Interspiritual *Shmita*	169
8 Ramadan Adjacent	175
9 Interspiritual Yom Kippur	179
10 Good Shabbos	185

CONCLUSION The Interspiritual Jewish Manifesto	*191*
Acknowledgements	*195*
Appendix: What You Can Do	*199*
Notes	*203*
Bibliography	*215*
Original Art	*225*
Author Bio	*227*

FOREWORD

Dear Lauren,

Your book is exceptional. I am not an expert in these fields, but can recognize expertise, and this is it, and much more. It is exploratory in the best sense; that is, you explore content, invite the reader into the exploration, and provide questions for which you and the reader have no single answers.

It is personal and professional; it includes you and your thought process, based partly on your professional roles as a teacher, and other roles you have played with the topic. Indeed, you are both a learner and teacher. You take everyday experiences with students, readings with a wide range of scholars, and observations on the issues of the day; these become exercises for your own thinking process. In this, it is an intellectual autobiography and draws upon disparate in-depth interactions with students and scholars.

The book is scholarly, you have profound knowledge of several subjects, and an ability to write in a both a learned and erudite way that is also popular in its outreach. The writing is excellent, in some places, exceptionally so; it is "elegant" in the same ways that some architects use the word, to describe a seemingly simple solution to a complex problem, like a "director's chair."

You have a vision which is especially compelling during these times. Once there was Judaism, then there was Judaism in response to antisemitism and the Holocaust, so that today the Jewish experience is too often taught and learned through hatred of Jews and fear of them as the other. To understand Judaism as a form of hatred "inside out" too often presents it as a reactive category.

During these times, more than ever, we need systems of beliefs and behaviors that are rooted in social justice visions and intercultural practices, and why not the Jews? Judaism is ideally positioned to claim itself as the belief system that is socially just. Instead of young people decreasing in their identifications with Judaism, I can imagine young people wanting to identify with Judaism - indeed, thronging to Judaism, as a faith institution of choice, among the others.

Part of the appeal of this thinking is that you are thinking about "a world that does not exist." I see you as an intellectual force advancing the new Judaism or "new strategies for Judaism," thus inviting the question "what is the new Judaism?" or "what are the new strategies?" You provide some of the answers and also some of the questions. In this, there are people who will be drawn to Judaism because it is a more multicultural vision than other spiritual traditions.

When asked about the new Judaism, your book contributes to this vision as a (1) field of practice (2) subject of study and (3) form of pedagogy that includes teaching and learning. Apparently, you have more intellect to cover in another book for which the present one is a preface.

I offer every encouragement.

Thanks for sharing.

Barry Checkoway

INTRODUCTION

INTERSPIRITUAL JUDAISM: A VISION

God was in this place and I, I did not know.
Genesis 28:16

Twenty-five years ago, I called an interfaith seminary. The secretary who answered the phone shared her enthusiasm for the program. As I wondered aloud if becoming an interfaith minister was a betrayal of my Jewish identity, she told me she was Jewish and added, "But Judaism is too small to fit all of me. I am so much more." She loved her Jewish culture, she said, but she couldn't belong to Judaism-only without shrinking who she was. Her experience was not uncommon. Over the years, I thought about what she meant. I believe it is not Judaism that was too small for her -if anything, Judaism is too big! - but *the worldview* through which it was given.

Judaism is a religion, a culture, and an ethnicity. As a religion, it includes beliefs about what is true (such as monotheism, the belief in one God), behaviors about how to live, and a community of belonging. As a religion, Judaism centers around a covenant with God (One) based on a set of divine laws. The cultural, legal *(halachic)* and spiritual traditions that define Judaism can take a lifetime to study. The body of scripture alone includes the Tanakh (Torah, Prophets, Writings) and the Talmud which includes rabbinic writings, Mishnah, Gemara, and other ways of interpreting the laws' applications. And there are thousands of books published each year about Judaism.

Not all Jews are religious. There are numerous denominations within Judaism. E.g., there are Humanistic Jews who don't believe in God, and Messianic Jews who believe in Christ. There are Jews who have replaced Judaism with another religion or added it to Judaism. Like other world religions, Judaism influences and is influenced by human culture. As Jews interact with the outside world these influences make it difficult to reduce Judaism (or any religion) to an isolated subject of study. Thus, while this book talks about Judaism as a religion, bear in mind that religion cannot be separated from its cultural dimensions.

George E. Mendenhall (1916-2016), the preeminent American biblical scholar of his day, defined religion as *"the complex of values that determine the function of persons and social organizations in cultural systems."* In the introduction to his course, A Field Theory of Religious Systems, which he delivered at The University of Michigan in 1979-80, Mendenhall said, "Any respectable and fruitful study of any religious system other than the most simple and primitive must of necessity be interdisciplinary." (Courtesy of Gary Herion, Mendenhall's former student and Professor Emeritus of Religious Studies at Hartwick College and George's son, Stan Mendenhall, for this definition.) In short, Judaism (and all our world's great religions) are anything but 'too small'.

In living, dynamic systems like Judaism, there is always more to learn, study, interpret, and practice. Yet even Judaism can *seem small* when the consciousness of humanity expands and the forms for experiencing it lag. This gap can result in our religions *feeling* small. When consciousness evolves, a new worldview is needed. With it, we need new forms, new institutions, new frames of reality for growing with our religions. In short, I believe the interfaith seminary secretary's worldview, the big story through which she constituted her world, had outgrown the worldview or big story through which Judaism had been presented to her.

When we "contain multitudes," as Walt Whitman once said, we might no longer fit into the boxes, or worldviews, we've outgrown.[1] Religions and legacy institutional leaders have been operating for decades from such boxes, or worldviews, while some people are experiencing a more rapid development of human consciousness, often spurred by current events. Many of the forms through which we experience and practice religion, indeed, through which we make meaning of the world, need to catch up to the planet's emerging and expanding worldview. Judaism has always adapted to historical changes, and it needs to adapt once again.

This book is about reimagining Judaism (or any religion) in the age of our newly emerging, expanding consciousness. At a time of declining interest in or satisfaction with religion, the time is ripe for a new worldview through which we can make meaning if our religions are to survive. And the survival of our religions is at stake. The divisiveness in the world today is tearing apart those who profess a belonging to and an identity with a religion. In the Jewish community today, this division is acute. The good news is that many Jews are now talking about "what it means to be Jewish in a fractured world." But is the fracture in the world, in us, or both?

This book is for Jews who feel torn within themselves or from their communities. So, what might this *new* worldview be and how will Judaism (and Jews) adapt to it?

Worldviews

Worldviews are the big stories through which we experience and make sense of the world. In *Cosmos and Psyche*, author Richard Tarnas writes,

> *Our worldview is not simply the way we look at our world. It reaches inward to constitute our innermost being, and outward to constitute the world. It mirrors but also reinforces and even forges the structures... and possibilities of our interior life. It deeply configures our psychic and somatic experience, the patterns of our sensing, knowing and interacting with the world. No less potently, our worldview ~ our beliefs and theories, our maps, our metaphors, our myths, our interpretive assumptions ~ constellates our outer reality, shaping and working the world's malleable potentials in a thousand ways of subtly reciprocal interaction. Worldviews create worlds.*

In *Worldly Philosopher: The Odyssey of Albert O. Hirschman*, historian Jeremy Adelman tells the story of political economist Albert Hirschman as he came of age during the fall of the Weimar Republic and Hitler's rise. Having become aware of the importance of worldviews in prewar Germany for how they create and change worlds, Albert bolted down the hall of his childhood home exclaiming to his sister, *"Weiss Du was? Vati hat keine Weltanschauung!"* (*You know what? Daddy has no worldview!*)

We may not always be conscious of our worldview, let alone others', but that doesn't mean we don't have one. Being aware of our worldviews and of their positives and negatives can make us more effective in living from their values. Since worldviews literally create worlds, they can be both the cause of problems and the source of solutions. Being aware of our worldviews can also help us decide if, when, and how we want to live with other or additional values calling us to create a new world.

We can explore and understand different worldviews when we ask these philosophical, existential questions: *What is the nature of reality? What is our relationship to ourselves, to others, to nature, to spirituality? What can be known and how? What is good, true, and beautiful? How shall we live?* While our religions inform some of these answers, they are part of worldviews, not equivalent to them. Many thinkers have contributed to our understanding of worldviews. Today, three major worldviews dominate Western cultures. They are referred to as the traditional (premodern), modern, and progressive (postmodern) worldviews. The name for the new worldview that is currently emerging will be addressed later.

The following chart summarizes aspects of the three dominant worldviews, courtesy of Worldview Journeys founder, Annick de Witt, Ph.D.

Traditional worldview	**Modern worldview**	**Postmodern worldview (Progressive)**
Theistic, dualistic, transcendent view of reality	Objectified materialistic, mechanistic view of reality	Pluralistic, fragmented relativistic view of reality
Knowledge through tradition, convention, scripture (literalism, dogmatism)	Knowledge through empirical science, rationality, logic (positivism, scientism)	Knowledge through qualitative modes of knowing (social constructivism)
Social self	Independent self	Authentic self
Traditional values (ie. solidarity, security, discipline, service, faith, conformity)	Individualistic values (ie. achievement, hedonism, success, status, power, fun)	Post-material values (ie. self expression, imagination openness to change)
Emphasis on family, social roles and rules, law and order	Emphasis on the future, belief in progress, optimism	Emphasis on deconstruction of narratives, social justice
Nature as meaningful, divinely constructed order (God's creation)	Nature as instrumental, objectified, resource for exploitation	Nature as inner source, oppressed voice or entity, larger system

Since the Enlightenment, according to de Witt, and McIntosh, the modern worldview which values truth, rationality, objectivity, science and technology has served to mitigate the contrast between the values of the traditional and postmodern worldviews. However, despite its advances in progress and technology, the modern worldview has come under attack by those who hold traditional and postmodern worldviews. The failures of the modern worldview include the growing economic wealth gap, ecological crisis, and lack of meaning and life-affirming values, all of which have led to an epidemic of alienation, loneliness, stress, and ill-health.

Since most Western people tend to identify with one of these three dominant generalized worldviews, the gap between traditional (cultural right) and postmodern or progressive worldviews (cultural left) keeps growing. This explains the intense polarization in our society today. The space between polarities leaves a vacuum. It causes people on both sides to become more radical, and no one can agree on what is true. We now live in what integral philosopher, Ken Wilber, calls a post-truth world. Without truth, or what historian Tim Snyder calls "facticity," we stand to lose our freedom. (Snyder claims freedom depends on sovereignty, social mobility, unpredictability, facticity, and solidarity.) The pushback, the antithesis of the dialectic of evolution, fills this void until, as Hegel taught, a synthesis emerges.

It seems odd to think that the collective consciousness of humanity is expanding when people are veering towards their polarity of exclusivity, isolationism, and tribalism. Afterall, where is the expansion of values in the collective consciousness when people allow their government to rid their communities of social justice, erase history from public and digital spaces, dismiss civil servants without cause, intentionally foment violence, weaponize education, rupture international relationships, reject science, deport innocent immigrants, attack civil rights, and more? These actions are expressions of the pushback against the energy from which the "new" will emerge. When those pushing back gain power, autocracy can and does result.

It is critical to acknowledge that such authoritarian actions are part of a *religious nationalism* that is rising not only in the US but all around the world. Americans are not immune to the spread of fear that leads to insularity and isolationism when coupled with religious nationalism.[2] We see it in the growing power of Christian Nationalists in America,[3] political Zionists in Israel (policies that expel, maim or kill Palestinians), Christian Nationalists in Hungary, Majoritarian Buddhists in Myanmar, and Islamist Muslims in Arab nations, etc.

As the United States turns increasingly towards its own version of ethno-fascism and particularly white supremacy, Christian Nationalism tracks to dominate American culture[4] and possibly in a violent form.[5] Christian Nationalists openly aim to keep people of other religions (including Catholics and non-conforming Christians) out of the halls of American government.[6] The move to isolationism and insularity today is a form of resistance or pushback to humanity's spiritual growth. This regression, this backwards motion, is part of the evolutionary process of spiritual growth as our culture develops a new big story. We are in the throes of resistance to the formation of a new worldview.

This global resistance to humanity's cultural evolution manifests today in authoritarian governments, oligarchic economies, and the different forms of religious nationalism. It gathers power until a preferred alternative, a dialectic synthesis, emerges. This synthesis must be holistic. When asked what gift each religion brings to the world, Rabbi Zalman Shachter-Shalomi told the following story with Judaism as the example to explain a holistic understanding:

> *I believe that Gaia is whole and that every religion is like a vital organ of the planet. You cannot say that Earth can be alive with only the heart or with only the kidneys or with only the guts. It needs to have the whole thing. So, if, for instance, I was to say, 'We [Judaism/Jews] are the liver'... if we're going to be a good liver, then the heart will be able to mend, the lungs will be able to mend, and so on and vice versa. If [other organs/religions] will be able to renew, Christianity or Islam or Buddhism, in their own way so that it'll be a vitally*

contributory element to the wholeness of life on this planet, that's wonderful. [7]

Authoritarian leaders eventually fail to consolidate power when it's used to deaden humanity, or what historian Tim Snyder calls "Kirpa". Just as the human body needs diverse organs to live and as the planet needs biodiversity to flourish, so too does the culture of humanity need spiritual diversity to thrive. Each religion contributes to the whole. Without inclusivity and belonging, there can be no diversity. Without diversity, there can be no affirming of life (what Snyder calls "Liebe").

Just as children outgrow clothes and need new ones, we too need new forms and new frames for seeing the world. We need a new worldview. New forms -institutions, systems, measures, technologies, models, policies, etc.- will reflect the values of this newly emerging worldview. So, while it is a tumultuous time, it is also a promising one. The conflicting values and culture wars, indeed, what Annick de Witt calls a "battle of worldviews," will synthesize in new forms that eventually harmonize the core values of preceding worldviews. The dialectic process of growth in human consciousness includes resistance to it.

There is an evolutionary pressure, an urgent need, to grow from this backlash into our next big story or worldview. This urge will yield the new forms needed. The prior forms against which religious nationalists are rebelling are no longer adequate, but neither are the chaotic anti-forms to replace them. The newly emerging consciousness has been called different names by various scholars: *Integral Spirituality, Integral Consciousness, Post-postmodernism,* and *Integrative Worldview.* I call it the *Interspiritual Age* to capture its place in history.

The integral worldview includes a holistic/unified spiritual-evolutionary view of reality. According to de Witt, knowledge from this worldview will be acquired not only by convention (traditional worldview), empirical methods (modern worldview), and qualitative ways of knowing (postmodern worldview) but by integration or a mix of different methods guided by "pragmatism and critical realism." Universal values driving this worldview include the search for truth and wisdom, self-actualization, cultural evolution to solve global problems and an emphasis on global peace and compassion.

Whatever name sticks to this emerging worldview, it is becoming evident in different parts of society as new ideas contribute to its rise. My focus here is on the way our religions, in particular, Judaism, will show up in our daily lives as we create new forms to support a new vision or worldview. As Professor Erin K. Wilson, University of Groningen, said,
"Religion is...an inextricable part of the human experience. That is why understanding what religion means and does for people in their daily lives, as part of their lived realities, matters." (The Changing Nature of Religion in Today's World, June 9th, 2023) One often underappreciated influence on the way our lived reality of religion is experienced is the interfaith movement. It has positively impacted our society in ways we don't see so I offer a quick review.

From Interfaith to Interspiritual

The interfaith movement officially began in Chicago in 1893 with the first Parliament of World Religions (PWR). In 1993, the 100-year anniversary, PWR resumed its commitment to interfaith awareness with renewed enthusiasm. Since then, it has held global meetings in Cape Town (1999), Barcelona (2004), Melbourne (2009), Salt Lake City (2015), Toronto (2018), and Chicago (2023), with the next Parliament planned in 2027.

Local and global interfaith works, spurred by the Parliament, are leading us to the coming Interspiritual Age. In the United States, we can see it in *Interfaith America*, founded by Eboo Patel, where college students learn about each other's religions thus inspiring them to learn their own.[9] We see it as *Interfaith Alliance* supports America's multi-faith democracy and when Auburn Seminary's clergy of different faiths learn and share strategies for social change. We see it in The Interfaith Leadership Council of Metro Detroit's *Religious Diversity Journeys* program for public middle school students to visit different worship sites, meet clergy, and learn about the religions practiced there.[10] We see it in a North Carolina school district's social studies curriculum and *Religion*

Matters website to help social studies teachers teach *about* our world's religions.[11] We see it in *The Tanenbaum Center's* programs for teachers, healthcare providers, workplace managers, and peacemakers around the world as they learn how to transform conflicts steeped in beliefs, behaviors and communities into opportunities for growth.[12]

We see it in other countries such as Canada's *Encounter World Religions* program for teachers, employers, and police to learn about different religions and why. We see it in Europe's commitment to religion education (RE) and philosophy courses for public high school students. We see it in the North American Interfaith Network's annual conference to bring together interfaith advocates from Canada, the US, and Mexico. We saw it in the former *Tony Blair Faith Foundation* that brought teachers and students of different faiths together. We see it in KAICIID, an international intergovernmental organization promoting intercultural and interreligious dialog. These are just some of many interfaith efforts in our world. Reading this list might make one wonder why, by now, we don't have peace in the world. Today, it is not enough to teach *about* different religions. We need to engage more fully with others who practice them or hold their beliefs and expose ourselves to interspiritual experiences - not instead of identifying with our religions, but in addition to.

According to sociologist Christian Smith, author of *Why Religions Went Obsolete: The Demise of Traditional Faith in America,* the title says it all. Smith's current prediction echoes the French Jesuit priest, geologist and paleontologist, Pierre Teilhard de Chardin, who attempted to reconcile Christianity with the science of evolution. In the early 1950s, de Chardin predicted that for religions to survive and evolve, they must undergo a "spiritualization" toward unity, becoming, in effect, interspiritual. Similarly, in the late 1990s, the American Catholic monk and author, Brother Wayne Teasdale, also predicted an interspiritual age where religions will transcend division and reach a shared, planetary consciousness. Simply put, our world's religions, to survive and thrive, must become interspiritual. The way we practice and teach religion will matter.

While some seminaries offer courses to clergy-in-training on interfaith topics[13], such material rarely reaches teachers of students in the religious schools. Today, most teachers of religious after-school educational programs, i.e., Saturday and Sunday schools, are college students or volunteer members of the affiliated institution. Most lack higher education in their religion let alone in others. In religious day schools, teachers may get additional training in their religion, but interfaith literacy is not considered a priority, so the work of interfaith educators is largely dismissed. But, as students are exposed to interfaith education in public schools and colleges through some of the organizations named above, we can hope future generations will benefit from their experience, bringing interfaith awareness to younger students.

For religions to survive and thrive, I believe interfaith education and interspiritual experience need to be part of a religion's educational program. People are hungry for spirituality and connection, for something sturdy enough to hold them but not so strict as to confine them. Our tribes, the religious teachings and communities with which we identify, can fill this need by opening up to each other. Thus, the interfaith movement has been laying a foundation for the adoption of a worldview in sync with the coming Interspiritual Age.

I see a time when all the world's religions are celebrated from our newly emerging consciousness, one that transcends the negatives of ethnic tribalism and nationalism. I see people engaging with religions from an enthusiasm found by recognizing the universal spiritual truths in all our religions while appreciating and respecting the uniqueness of each one.

Integral philosopher Steve McIntosh writes that, *"The culture of integral spirituality is found in the growing agreement about the importance of spiritual experience."*[8] I am not calling for syncretic blending of different religions but for renewed interest in learning from, with and alongside others to deepen our own understanding of spiritual experience. Thus, the interspiritual movement will override limitations of polite pluralism (the postmodern worldview) and reveal unifying spiritual principles of all faiths (integral worldview). Our collective consciousness will gain energy from those religions that embrace and value common spiritual truths and experiences. In short, the antidote to religious nationalism and that which can help us evolve our collective consciousness through today's polarization lies with interfaith education and interspiritual experiences. It means celebrating and teaching religion with other religions.

Ironically, the way out of the religious nationalism that pulls us back is through religion - not one but all. We need each other, all of us from different tribes, to experience this interspiritual form of religion, *socially*. Our world has diverse spiritual traditions and practices through which to form faith, develop morally, and live spiritually and our social solidarity will come when we respect all our religions, develop friendships across faith lines, and learn to learn from each other. The Interspiritual Age, a flourishing of spiritual and social solidarity, is underway. It is a natural extension of interfaith dialogue, multiculturalism, multi-faith prayer, interreligious study, interfaith social justice coalitions, and of course, interfaith families.

My authority to share this reimagination, this new vision of Judaism for the Jewish community and as an example for others of where their religions may soon or already are heading, comes from training in modern rabbinic studies and interfaith ministry[14], experience leading a Jewish and interfaith-oriented congregation, teaching at a synagogue's after-school religious program, running an independent Sunday School for Jewish and Jewish Interfaith families, designing educational programs on religion for international students and for the general public, serving on the board of an interfaith round table, attending numerous conferences on interfaith education and activism, participating in a professional association of religion educators, and serving on a committee for religion education in public life, as well as 40 years in an interfaith relationship and family.

Prior to this work, I earned an interdisciplinary doctoral degree that resulted in teaching children of all ages, college students, teachers, and trainers in a range of subjects including educational methods, ethics, psychology, philosophy, philosophy for children, gaming-simulation (the future's language), art and Judaism. When I studied Hegel with Professor Howard Adelman (z'l), I began to see the world through the eyes of a *philosopher of history*. Like others, Hegel, believed human consciousness develops toward higher states with an impulse towards the Good. This idea, also found in Judaism, forms the underlying assumption of this book. We evolve. To survive, we now need each other.

Since religion education is a sector of society where spiritual maturity is a goal and is often devoted to ethical living or faith formation, this book argues for experiencing, practicing, celebrating, studying and teaching religion from the perspective of a new worldview. We can ask: Are our religions serving us in ways that help us evolve (implying towards something better/Good) or are they part of the problem? Since this book is about Judaism, we can ask: Is Judaism, with its brand of nationalism (political Zionism), current Ashkenazi-centric leadership, Israel-centric Jewish education (in Israel and in the Diaspora), and Holocaust-centric identity holding Jews back (wherever they are) from needed growth in consciousness? And if so, what are the ways that Jews can grow with Judaism beyond this ethno-centric phase?

This book is for those who want to connect to religion with *new* forms. It is for Jews who want a new frame for Judaism. I invite us to consider a form of Judaism that does not require us to shrink who we are to fit into a box -be it traditional, modern, postmodern, or another worldview - that we may be outgrowing. Religions need a new worldview with a bigger story to hold us and our world's many rich traditions. As Shane Burley and Ben Lorber point out in *Safety Through Solidarity,* "The Jewish story has been told with what Magda Teter calls a "limited vocabulary," where too often, only our suffering is deemed worthy to recall." (p.324) However, Judaism in a form that highlights social solidarity with multiple (non-nationalist) religious communities, can expand our vocabulary and allow us to see ourselves not as victims but as evolutionary agents of social change and spiritual maturity. This new worldview does not replace the values of prior worldviews but integrates their best parts. This then is the Interspiritual Age. Growing, evolving, maturing, expanding our consciousness requires seeing through new inclusive and transcending forms which we are called to create.

This book consists of short chapters, or essays, that can be read in any order. They are organized into three major themes: 1) Belong to the World, 2) Bring your Tribe, and 3) Celebrate. The first two parts are philosophical, reflective, and auto biographical. The last part, based on personal experimentation, provides ideas, even resources, for practicing a new vision of Judaism. It's a start and by no means complete.

PART ONE: Belong to the World asks us to belong to a state of mind, a "World", a new level of consciousness with a widening worldview. It refers to a time and a place in our history and in our minds that I call the *Interspiritual Age*. I ask us to engage with our religions and all religions from this place and to bravely overcome inner and outer obstacles to reach it. In this way, we develop the foundation for a new vision for Judaism and for new forms of experiencing it.

PART TWO: Bring Your Tribe is a call to my fellow Jews, members of our tribe. Here, I speak about Jewish identity, Judaism in Israel and in the Diaspora. To *bring your tribe* means to bring the *teachings of your religion* into a new reality frame. It means recognizing our resistance to a new worldview and what comes after the regression. It means looking forward to how we might integrate our religion's core values into a new form for a new age. This will affect how Judaism is practiced and taught, as well as to whom, by whom, and with whom. Judaism's current attachment to political Zionism and the policies of the nation-state of Israel make it difficult for some members of the tribe to decouple from this older form. While bearing witness and holding compassion for all those experiencing pain on all sides of the conflict is important, we also need interspiritual activism to help bring Jewish thought and teachings and our Jewish Family into the new "World" or worldview.

PART THREE: Become Interspiritually Jewish, offers a peek into how we can become Jewish in the Interspiritual Age. This means *including and transcending* (Ken Wilber's term for evolution's process) our older forms of Judaism. I give examples of how Judaism might be celebrated in the Interspiritual Age through various Jewish holidays. Of course, our religions are much more than their festivals. However, holidays tend to be familiar to both religious practitioners and non-practitioners and so, for my purposes, they serve as entry points for reimagining religion, in this case, Judaism, in the Interspiritual Age. This section provides resources for practicing what it might be like to be Jewish in a new, interspiritual way. It is certainly a big part of what we need now.

While the examples in this section have been tested, they may seem dated given recent changes (too rapid for some, too slow for others) in the Jewish community, especially since October 7, 2023. Nonetheless, they serve as suggestions and inspiration for the future of Judaism in the Interspiritual Age. Indeed, these versions of celebration prove the point that the new forms into which religions morph often unfurl through catastrophic historical events. These newer forms offer a framework into which we can imagine growing spiritually and interspiritually with our tribes, religious traditions, and with others.

Ideally, when the Interspiritual Age is in full swing, we will celebrate our holidays with those of other religions, and they will be celebrating theirs with us. For interfaith families, this is already happening and we can learn from their experience. The path is clear. We need the pavement.

PART ONE

BELONG TO THE WORLD

Belong to the World Bring Your Tribe is the title of this book and my personal motto. When we belong to a tribe, identity forms around a family, ethnic group, religious community, and even a nation-state. Tribalism can dominate our identity with "tribal" values such as love of family, attachment to a land, and patriotism for a country. Yet, when these values pathologize into extremes of racism and nationalism, we need to release the parts that no longer serve us and heal the harm they've caused as we bring the healthy parts of tribal values into a new worldview where they are synthesized with newer values that expand and harmonize disparate parts. In our new worldview, we *belong to a tribe(s) and to the World*. Tribe becomes part of something greater, not an end unto itself. To *bring your tribe* is to integrate the best of ethnocentrism with the best of world-centrism, where *all* our world's tribes serve a bigger story. Each tribe's wisdom contributes value to this new, bigger story.

The need for a new worldview lies in our perceived life conditions. Today's life conditions reflect real problems for which we lack realistic solutions, unavailable through the ethno-centric worldview held by religions operating from the formerly dominant worldview. But a *world-centric morality*, perhaps a universe or cosmos-centric worldview is even better, can help us develop the shared responsibility we need for climate change, wealth inequality, war, and other global problems. We need a groundswell of world-centric morality. How refreshing it was to learn that Pope Leo XIV convened thought leaders across religions to promote a covenant of humanity *"founded not on power but on care; not on profit but on gift; not on suspicion but on trust."* (Claire Giangrave, "Pope Leo urges covenant," *Religion News Service,* September 12, 2025)

Tribalists turned nationalists tend to perceive life as threatening and spirit-controlled, resulting in magical thinking. They find safety in the tribe more than in shared humanity. But our global problems cannot be solved from such a frame. We must choose: *Will we allow a single tribe's religious nationalism to be the spiritual imperialist over all others? Or will we promote all religions and their unique contributions to thrive in a wider, larger frame of consciousness? Will we belong, freely and equally together, in the Interspiritual Age?* If we are to improve conditions of life to save our planet and all people, we need a shared worldview without egos or ethnic groups dominating from the center. This means creating a sense of *belonging* to a larger story with a bigger consciousness to hold it.

Belonging Versus Inclusion

For world-centric thinking and a culture of solidarity to take hold (so we can solve our global problems together), we all need to *belong.* To not belong is to be disconnected from others, to experience the dis-ease of loneliness, as documented by British journalist, Johann Hari, in *Lost Connections*. Even the former US Surgeon General Dr. Vivek Murthy called out loneliness as an epidemic of the West. How then do we achieve the interconnectedness of belonging?

John A. Powell, internationally recognized expert in civil rights, civil liberties, structural racism, housing, poverty, and democracy and the director of the *Othering and Belonging Institute* at University of California-Berkeley, claims that belonging means more than being included. When we are included, we don't necessarily belong. The invitation is temporary, he says. Inclusivity doesn't mean we are part of co-creating. It just means we get to show up to someone else's party. True belonging is showing up not as a guest but as a co-creator. Belonging means having a voice in co-creating the vision for our shared world. Belonging to the World challenges us to overcome the instinct to isolate with our tribes and live in an ethno-centric frame, perhaps especially when we feel threatened.

Our voices must give form to a compelling story of belonging to the World - *for everyone.* That story must be as inspirational as the story of the Exodus for Jews, the Hijrah for Muslims, the birth of Jesus for Christians, the birth of Krishna for Hindus, etc. It must be a universal story in which we all see ourselves.[15] What this story *cannot* be is a vision of one religion/nation dominating others. The stories we tell our children will matter. *Will we belong to tribes that belong to a World to be shared by all humanity?*

Bring Your Tribe
We succeed at "belonging to the world" when we "bring our tribes". Progressives may forge ahead and leave traditionalists behind but if so, they will lack the ability to develop the power to institute their programs while traditionalists may resist the evolutionary pressure to change and thus miss out on the creative energy of new growth. Neglecting members of our tribes will result in an evolutionary undertow that could drown us all. But what if we opt to belong to the world AND bring our tribes?

Like moving into a new house, we bring what is meaningful and **fits and let go of what we no longer need. We integrate what we are preserving as we innovate in the new space. We cull and revise as we inhabit our new home, our new Age, our new worldview. When our tribes belong to something bigger, to a more expanded level of consciousness, we all have space to thrive.**

Although this book is focused on the religious sphere, to "belong to the World," new forms for a new worldview are and will emerge in all sectors of society. It is refreshing to see efforts now taking place that aim to bring our tribes with us. In the political sphere, *Braver Angels,* a New York based nonprofit bringing 'red' and 'blue'

Americans together to depolarize our politics, is adding chapters around the country. Similarly, *DEMOS (Democracy Dialogs)*, an open-source project to address low trust in democracy and difficulties in conflict resolution and communication, is being adopted by local communities. In the mental health sphere, *Integrative Community Therapy and Solidarity Care,* a nonprofit with a successful method for healing soul pain and collective suffering that was started in Brazil, is now spreading to the United States.

Belong to the World Bring Your Tribe invites us to co-create a new relationship with ourselves, each other, and our tribes. We are called to create new forms to support an emerging level of consciousness. To belong to the world of an Interspiritual Age is to discern what's valuable, healthy, and worth preserving from our traditions while removing what is unhealthy or objectionable.

Making these discernments, we create *"a common culture of spiritual experience that honors diverse traditions but also endeavors to discover those aspects of spirituality...around which new levels of cultural solidarity can arise."*[16] In short, interfaith education honors our diverse and separate traditions while interspiritual experiences develop our greater unity and sense of social solidarity.

When I invite us in Part One to Belong to the World, this is what I'm talking about. **World with a capitalized W refers to the Interspiritual Age** where religions are embraced with a new vision. As we evolve, so too do our institutions, our holders of the forms. Indeed, we become managing agents in our development, not passive recipients. As such, we are no longer bound to identify with our religion based on *how it was* but free to engage based on *how it can be.* Hallelujah!

In our Interspiritual Age, we solve problems that our prior stages of consciousness failed to adequately address. With this shift, we intentionally shape the future and empower the past (our ancestors) with a voice but not a veto.[17] A future that has not yet happened is one which -through positive freedom (Snyder) and reflective freedom (Stewart) - our imagination blooms. In some ways, this book is a nod to the late Walter Brueggeman, renowned American Christian scholar and theologian, for whom the biblical prophets were poets who saw *"their contemporary world differently...[through] tradition and imagination."*[18] We have plenty of tradition. What we need is imagination.

(1)
GETTING UNSTUCK

I agreed to speak at *The Unstuck Conference: Reviving the Movement for Social Justice, Human Dignity and the Environment* (organized by Pastor Joe Summers in 2016) because I thought I had a lot to say. But when I sat down to write, I was "stuck." Here's what I learned about getting "unstuck."

I grew up in a religiously conservative and politically liberal Jewish household. I attended a Hebrew School every Monday, Wednesday, and Sunday. My family went to Sabbath Services, so I was at the synagogue on Saturdays, too. When I joined a Jewish Youth Group, I was there Saturday evenings as well. I went to Jewish camps in the summer. I lived on a religious *kibbutz* in Israel during high school. I attended Hebrew University in Jerusalem for a year of college. I thought I would join the Israeli army, marry an Israeli, and live on a *kibbutz*. Would you be surprised if I told you, it didn't work out that way?

So, what happened?

I fell in love with someone who is not Jewish. God has a sense of humor. As a result, I was exposed to a different way of thinking about the world and my place in it. My marriage led me on a path of interfaith experiences. Over the years, I led a Jewish-Interfaith congregation, ran an alternative Hebrew School for children of Jewish and Jewish Interfaith families, served on the board of an Interfaith Round Table, designed interfaith multilogue programs, officiated interfaith weddings and coming of age ceremonies *(bar/bat/b-mitzvahs)*, organized religion tours and interfaith movie nights for students, coached interfaith couples, convened an adult Faith Club, Interfaith *Mussar* Club, and more. Along the way, my relationship with religion and my ideas about teaching developed in unexpected ways.

One such experience occurred at a special conference for aspiring Interfaith Educators that included Jews, Christians, and Muslims.[19] In one session, we were asked to go around the circle and each share our biggest fear about Interfaith. My immediate thought was, "I don't have any fear." Until David spoke.

David was 30 years old, training to be a rabbi, and the father of a one-year-old. His biggest fear was that his daughter might not identify with Judaism, that if she learned about other faiths, she might be attracted to them and identify with a different religion, different from his. When I heard David speak, I realized, "Uh-Oh, I do have a fear." So, I spoke up.

"My fear is just the opposite," I said. "I fear that if I don't expose my children and my students to interfaith opportunities, they'll identify too much with Judaism and get stuck; stuck in one religion and stalled in larger interspiritual development. For if there's one thing I learned on my journey, it was that interfaith engagement initiates spiritual growth." Learning about other faith traditions helps us get unstuck from our own. Sometimes we must cross a mental border and look at ourselves from the other side. And the corollary is also true. This process can work the other way around. Sometimes when we're out gathering spirituality from different traditions, we need to step back to interpret it. That's when our own religious roots can be helpful. Maybe they are strengthened by what we see that's different. Maybe they're challenged. Maybe we have changed.

At the same conference, we were also asked to meet separately with people from our own religion. All the Jews meet here, all the Christians there, all the Muslims somewhere. Since the Muslims were the most under-represented, if you weren't sure where to go, you were allowed to go with the Muslims. I almost did.

See, I was upset. In my experience, Judaism was so "we-they" and "us-them" oriented, so *over-identified* with itself that the Jewish community always seemed to be threatened, not just by the world outside but from within as well. Growing up, my community was threatened by my parents' divorce. Threatened by my brother's sexual orientation. Threatened by my inter-marriage. Threatened by any Otherness. So, I wasn't sure I belonged in an "all-only" Jewish group. But my loyalty led me there.

In the circle, I shared my disappointment in the Jewish community for not embracing interfaith education, interfaith marriage, and interfaith dialogue as *assets* rather than liabilities. I shared my disillusionment with Judaism for its ongoing harm done to Palestinians. This was something I could not tolerate. Then something unexpected happened. Immediately after the session, five people rushed over to me offering support and *wanting to understand* how I saw Judaism. Later, it hit me.

The very thing for which I'd been disappointed in my tradition — its reluctance to know and accept the Other — was keeping me from Judaism. Without realizing it, I'd been stuck in Interfaith but the willingness of fellow Jews to listen, released me — just as I released them from their fear of Interfaith. So how do we keep from getting stuck inside or outside our religions?

Psychoanalyst, Julia Kristeva, who studied "the stranger" both as an outsider and an insider, writes,

> *Strangely, the foreigner lives within us: he is the hidden face of our identity, the space that wrecks our abode, the time in which understanding and affinity founder. By recognizing him within ourselves, we are spared detesting him in himself, a symptom that precisely turns "we" into a problem...The foreigner comes in when the consciousness of my difference arises, and he disappears when we all acknowledge ourselves as foreigners.*[20]

Over-Identifying with any one religion, combination of religions, or the exclusion of all religions can keep us from seeing the Other in ourselves. If we keep walls so thick and high, that we only see the foreigner on the outside, we rob ourselves of acknowledging the foreigner within and growing as a result. We need not throw away religions but often, religion educators are consumed with ensuring *Continuity* and securing *Identity* whenever they feel threatened. And, it seems, they always feel threatened. Thus, they encourage what I call over-identification, an obsession with religious and ethnic identity that can turn into nationalism. People with an ethnocentric worldview often feel persecuted; it is part of that worldview. One way to counter over-identification is to shift (not replace) the value placed on "identity" to something else. I propose "integrity." Paradoxically, our religious traditions provide the wisdom for doing so.

To be a person of integrity is to be responsible and more. This takes inner work. Jewish sages teach that the Hebrew word for responsibility, *achrayut,* gives clues as to its deeper meaning. Alan Morinis, in *Everyday Holiness,* says the root *achar* means "after," implying we consider the consequences of our decisions before we make them. The same root with a different vowel, *acher,* means "other." It implies bearing the burden of caring for the Other.[21] Emphasizing the responsibility of integrity over (not instead of) identity, comes closer to what religions are good at — allowing us to make the world better by considering how actions affect others now and later. In the world-centric (and integral) worldview, this includes all others.

In a study on Jewish identity whose authors defined being Jewish as *someone who stands up against antisemitism*, one of my students said, "Standing up against antisemitism doesn't make you Jewish, it makes you a good person." That is what I mean by integrity over identity. Living in the Interspiritual Age calls for teaching and upholding religions with new forms that embrace a wider set of values where integrity holds more weight than identity. Of course, identity matters but its responsibility is focused on the tribe whereas integrity opens our responsibility to members of our tribe *and of other tribes*, as well as to all species. Others include us, our tribes and all people, of all religions and ethnic groups. *Integrity over identity* is the first principle for belonging to the World.

In the context of current hostilities between Israel, a nation-state that claims to represent Jews around the world, whether active or estranged, are called to discern integrity and identity. Will integrity (informed by Jewish spiritual values and interspiritual values of all tribes) enable us to reclaim Judaism and humbly transcend our ethno-centric frame to belong to the World?

②
INTEGRAL AND INTERSPIRITUAL

FLASHBACK: I am sitting on the floor, a foot from the TV, turning channels. There is no remote, no recording device, no Internet. An animated human stick figure appears on the screen. The narrator explains that a human being will experience eight significant crises in their lifetime. Each will occur within certain stages of development around a major issue such as trust, identity, and intimacy. I sprint for pen and paper. At age 14, Erik Erikson gave me a map of my future in terms of psycho-social stages. *What other life maps, I wondered, were out there?*

Eventually, I discovered Hegel, the 19th century German philosopher who traced the evolution of human consciousness through its various stages. Just as I was eager to absorb Erikson's stages from childhood to adulthood, I sought to understand humanity through Hegel's *Phenomenology of Spirit*. Other philosophers have expanded on Hegel's ideas (Sri Aurobindo, Jean Gebser, Teilhard de Chardin, Robert Kegan, Ken Wilber, Steve McInstosh, Carter Phipps, etc.) to provide a rather hopeful map. To make better use of it, what follows are terms to help us navigate the terrain ahead.

INTEGRAL
Integral refers to the emerging level of consciousness now needed as the prior level meets its limitations. According to Ken Wilber, renowned integral philosopher, as we experience different levels of consciousness, each one handles more complexity than the one before. Thus, we are *still* growing. In fact, another characteristic of integral theory is that *evolution* drives this growth.

The evolution of human consciousness continually promises the possibility of new solutions to age-old problems. As Einstein said, no problem can be solved from the same level of consciousness that created it. We must grow to survive, to solve new threatening situations. The newest level of consciousness arising on the cultural scene with a growing critical mass is *integral consciousness,* a feature of the Interspiritual Age.

Can integral consciousness solve today's problems?

According to integral philosopher Steve McIntosh, yes. The values of an integral worldview help us address climate change, income inequality, diminishing resources, political polarization, etc. The outgoing dominant consciousness of rational materialism proved incapable of realistic solutions to these threats. But an integral worldview expands our values. We don't trade one worldview for another. We grow with our worldview. McIntosh lists features of the new consciousness as follows[22]:

- *new insight into the "internal universe" meaning the developing field of consciousness*
- *personal responsibility for the problems of the world*
- *renewed appreciation for the values held in previous stages of consciousness*
- *aspiration for the harmonization of science and religion*
- *appreciation for evaluating our problems through a dialectical process*
- *a world-centric morality that transcends the "us-them" thinking of previous stages of consciousness (for Wilber, cosmo-centric morality)*
- *compassion for all worldviews, even those that seem narrow-minded or ego-centric*
- *a revival of philosophy*
- *overcoming the culture war that results when two different worldviews clash*
- *a renewed insistence on achieving results (that are lasting and beneficial to all)*

Can we consciously develop into this integral consciousness?

Religions strive to answer metaphysical questions, so religion teachers and clergy can teach and lead in ways that grow our consciousness. Just as medical schools now teach integrative/holistic medicine to help patients improve their health, religious schools can teach integrative/holistic religion to help us develop spiritually.

If we choose to inhabit integral consciousness, then the field of religion education will reveal more "faith-rooted social justice" activities, "multi-faith education" for congregants, "interfaith dialogue" for students, "philosophy in the religious school classroom," and a "unifying narrative that incorporates science in religion lessons." Erikson clarifies the *individual*'s journey through psychosocial stages of growth while Hegel writes about the *collective* journey through culture's stages of consciousness. These developmental maps of what lie ahead for humanity give me hope that we can evolve consciously, grow spiritually, develop morally, and achieve peace globally.

INTERSPIRITUAL
Interspiritual is both the same and different from Interfaith.

Interfaith refers to *dialogue between people of different religions*. In interfaith dialogue, people share faith experiences, motivations, or practices to find common ground and foster both tolerance and appreciation of differences. *It also refers to marriage between people of different religious backgrounds.* Interfaith programs celebrate multiculturalism and religious diversity. Such dialogue involves members of different faiths.

Interspiritual, a term coined by Christian monk Wayne Teasdale, refers to the mystical core at the center of all the world's major spiritual traditions. *Interspiritual* describes inner-journey work that finds unity among the world's faith traditions while *Interfaith* describes dialogue and relationships that preserve diversity among them. Interspiritual experiences can result from, or lead to, interfaith activities and vice versa. Thus, the terms are often used interchangeably.

In *The Coming Interspiritual Age,* Kurt Johnson, a scientist ordained in three different spiritual traditions, suggests that *interspirituality* is so deeply rooted in the heart-experience of oneness that any creed, belief, background, or history that could cause separation between beings become secondary if not irrelevant.

When I led congregation *Jewbilation: Jewish Roots with Interfaith Wings,* for Jewish-Interfaith families, I also led an alternative, independent Sunday School. My program evolved over twenty years from Jewish and Interfaith to Interspiritual. The interfaith oriented program for learning a home religion that I developed could be a model for new forms of religious education in the Interspiritual Age. While the Unitarian Universalists include interfaith education for upper elementary and middle school students as part of their curriculum, it is not uniform throughout. And while 'Being Both' communities teach two religions as one identity throughout their curriculum,[23] they do not necessarily include additional faiths. In my sermons for the congregation I led, I intentionally included teachings from other religions alongside Jewish teachings. In addition, I brought adults of different faiths together to learn from Judaism and from each other and included lessons where my students learned from other faiths and the teachers of those religions.

If interfaith education was a regular part of a congregation's program, would it not convey the value of understanding each other's traditions? Through his synagogue, my friend, Phil Kruger, offers an optional online class for Jews and Christians on *Judaism and Christianity.* But this is rare. Most congregations do not offer let alone promote interfaith education for congregants. To make this a norm is to grow into our emerging worldview.

Below are examples of interfaith programs that have become institutions *among mainstream religions*. Some of these are what I call "side-by-side" experiences that are valuable opportunities for interfaith education. The locations are particularly interesting as they show where the new worldview is advancing.

House of Religions - Bern, Switzerland (2014) *The House of Religions Dialogue of Cultures is unique in the world as a place that unifies eight religious communities as well as a space dedicated to dialogue with the public under one roof.*

Abrahamic Family House - United Arab Emirates (2023) *AFH encompasses a mosque, a church, a synagogue and a Forum for gathering and dialogue.*

Tri-Faith Initiative - Omaha, Nebraska USA (2020) *Tri-Faith provides opportunities for Christians, Jews, and Muslims to learn from each other.*

The House of One - Berlin, Germany (under construction) *Jews, Christians, and Muslims are building a house of worship that brings a synagogue, a church, and a mosque under one roof linked by a communal room in the center of the building for worshippers and the public to learn more about their religions and each other.*

Global House of Friendship and Hope - Assisi, Italy (coming in 2026) *With support from religious leaders worldwide, Global House will offer an interactive museum and prayer space with immersion experiences for all faiths. It will invite visitors and members of all religions. Inspired by St. Francis, the project is led by Elijah Interfaith Institute, based in Jerusalem.*

Lama Foundation - Taos, New Mexico (since 1967) *Fosters "the awakening of consciousness" through spiritual practice with respect for all traditions and offers a spiritual community, educational facility, and retreat center. While there are other organizations like Lama, some virtual, I include this one for its longevity.*

With the Interspiritual Age, growing interest in multi-faith centers and interfaith education enriches our experience of religion and spirituality. To benefit from these experiences, deep and lasting friendships must also develop among people of different ethnicities, cultures, faiths or "tribes". These centers can provide opportunities for such friendships to form.

Friendship across faiths is an investment of time and energy that our faith leaders can encourage and demonstrate. But congregants, teachers, and students don't have to wait for the leaders. We can bring people of different faiths together in creative ways by meeting at interfaith programs and joining in activities together. See the Appendix for ideas. The following *Declaration of Friendship* from The Elijah Interfaith Institute is an example of the intention to develop such relationships.

DECLARATION OF FRIENDSHIP BY RELIGIOUS LEADERS

This Declaration is included with permission from
The Elijah Interfaith Institute

The Invitation

A world beset by fear of the other, indifference to the other and the widespread practice of hate, is a world in which no one can flourish. Now, more than ever, there is a need for greater unity, solidarity, common purpose and common action if we are to survive, and even more so if we are to flourish.

We therefore invite all religious leaders and teachers, and all people of faith, to cultivate a practice of friendship to others, across the divides that have kept many religious communities apart for centuries, respecting and embracing the difference of the religious other.

By practicing friendship, we grow together in the values for which our traditions have aspired, internally: respect, care, understanding, sharing, mutuality, and collaboration. We seek to change the ecology of relations, so that these qualities are also applied between diverse faith communities.

The Commitment

- As religious leaders and teachers of religious communities:

- We commit ourselves to practice, study, and encourage the practice of friendship across religions, extending it further to friendship beyond religion, and to our common home, as friends of the planet.

- We commit ourselves to set examples of interreligious friendship for our communities to follow.

- We commit ourselves to make visible gestures of friendship with leaders or members of another tradition.

- We commit ourselves to offer teachings that will uphold the value of friendship between religions and to disseminate them within our traditions.

- We commit ourselves to adapt this broad vision to the particular language and beliefs of our traditions and to their needs.

- We commit ourselves to establish and support educational frameworks and programs within our traditions and institutions that will provide opportunities to enhance genuine understanding of the religious other and the cultivation of friendship. We seek wiser and better-informed practice of our own faith as well as a wiser understanding of the faith of the other.

- We commit ourselves to create a climate that is conducive to the spread of friendship, including support for religious freedom

- Our commitment is expressed publicly by signing this declaration and recommending the practice of friendship both to leaders and to members of our communities, thereby making this declaration more than just another statement to be signed.

The Practice of Friendship

Friends learn to know each other, practice solidarity in times of need, and speak out for one another. Friendship is built on loving, sharing, listening, and respect. Friends pray for one another, deepening their friendship and lifting it up in the sight of God.

By risking friendships across deep differences, we can help to heal our world's divisions and conflicts. By entering the wisdom of each other's traditions, we can deepen mutual understanding and sensitivity.

Friendship across religions calls us to bring to light the higher virtues of our traditions and to practice them generously.

Friendship across religions can empower and give shape to a quest shared by many religions to work towards the preservation of the earth, our common home.

Friendship across religions allows us to draw on the accumulated wisdom and understanding of friendship found in our respective traditions and to make it available for the common good.

Finally, as we recognize from our experience, friendship is to be treasured for its own sake, and is a source of pleasure, joy, laughter, enrichment, inspiration, growth, self-understanding, trust, support, and personal flourishing.

③
EVOLUTIONARY AND NONDUAL

The word, **EVOLUTIONARY**, can be an adjective or a noun. It is sometimes used interchangeably with integral and interspiritual. As an adjective, *evolutionary* describes a process of development — not just biological but cultural. Unlike Darwin's view of biological evolution as a series of random accidents (natural selection), cultural evolution has an unmistakable direction and purpose. In this view of evolution, we are not just a different species. We are becoming a kinder, *better* species.[24] Planetary goodwill is supposedly on the rise, and it is not accidental. As a noun, an *evolutionary* is an active and conscious participant in the development of our consciousness and culture towards this better version.

Carter Phipps describes *evolutionaries* (plural) as people who take the idea of evolution seriously *and* personally; seriously, because it applies as much to culture as to the natural world, and personally, because individuals make choices in their everyday lives that determine their/our collective future. Psychohistorians such as Robert J. Lifton urged us as individuals to face our past to explain our present. Evolutionaries, however, encourage us to face our collective future to inspire better choices as we depart from our present.

Evolutionaries believe we can be instrumental in guiding our culture to ostensibly higher levels of expanded consciousness that benefit all beings and the planet. They are optimistic. If indeed a critical mass of people on the planet is poised to enter a stage of evolution in which humanity embraces universal values and acknowledges the dignity of all, perhaps we can solve the global problems that threaten our survival.

Will religion be part of this evolutionary process?

Theologically, religion shows signs of evolving. Author John Haught says *evolutionary spirituality* is not knowing God "up above" but knowing God "up ahead."[25] God is in the future. And the future is us. Carter Phipps writes,

Evolutionary spirituality...can awaken us to a universal process that is not neutral or inconsequential but more real and important than anything that happens in our individual lives. It can connect our own capacity of choice to a 13.7-billion-year process...playing out in the evolution of human consciousness and culture in our time. It can make us true believers again – not in heavenly deities or godly favors but in the positive, deeply spiritual nature of life and human potential. [26]

The evolutionary process Phipps describes is the bigger thing of which we can be a part *and* influence. What began with Darwin is only now coming into its fuller expression. French philosopher, Jesuit priest, and paleontologist, Pierre Teilhard de Chardin, saw it a century earlier when he predicted that only those religions willing to develop forms of their traditions that organically embrace the reality of an evolutionary worldview would survive. *How does religion embrace an evolutionary perspective?* The answer: organically, one person at a time. Including me.

In response to what integral philosophers might call "evolutionary pressure," I had to find a way to teach religion with students who did not fit the traditional model for Jewish education. To teach Judaism in the context of interfaith marriage, pluralism, and a globalizing culture meant the old model no longer fit. As more teachers, parents, and faith leaders (from all religions) find themselves in similar positions, they will feel the evolutionary pressure to revise their programs rather than force students into outdated, insufficient molds.

A newly emerging worldview puts evolutionary pressure on our religions to change. Each emergent worldview is, as Hegel told us, in a *dialectical relationship* to the one before it; each is an answer to the problems created by the previous dominant worldview. Each new stage of development simultaneously transcends *and* includes the values of the previous one. In short, worldviews are responses to changing life conditions. We need new responses for today's conditions. *How might the term nondual add to a new response to this conversation?*

NONDUAL means "not dual" so we need to understand dual. *Dual*ism refers to the two-ness of the world, such as opposites. Hot- Cold. Good- Evil. Left-Right. Light-Dark. Subject-Object. Joy-Grief. Dualism has roots in Cartesian philosophy with Renee Descartes' famous maxim, *I think, therefore I am*. His philosophy set in motion the Mind-Body distinction aka dualism that led the way for the Enlightenment and the growth of science where the scientist, separated from influencing the experiment, could discover objective truth. Dualism expresses itself in politics with the two-party system. It manifests in religion with the distinction between Divine and Human; God as separate from us and us as separate from God. Dualism is pervasive so that even when we say God is everywhere, from a dualist's frame of reality, we experience God as outside of us. Yet we yearn to be close to God *because* we feel separate. *But are we?*

Nondual refers to a worldview without dualism. Differentiated forms, opposites, diversity, etc. are present but they are unique expressions of an underlying Oneness. There is nothing but Oneness, which is ever changing, eternal, and infinite. Everything is everywhere all at once.

Nondual awareness is the state of mind, or mindfulness, of our true nature not as separate from but as part of this Oneness often called God. Thus, the dualism of dualism is an illusion. Not only are we close to God, but God dwells in each of us, and each of us in God. Once we cut through ego, the illusion that we are separated falls away. To hold a nondual philosophy is to see all theologies, including dualism, as expressions of the nondual. But it is also about living in the world of duality that expresses it. Let me quote Jay Michaelson at length on this point,

There is little separating the non-dualistic philosophies of Judaism from those of Hinduism, Buddhism, and other traditions—not nothing, but little. Nonduality, if true, is necessarily a universal truth, and all schools and teachers are but skillful means of apprehending it. However...nonduality does not erase the world in a hazy cloud of oneness... The general takes the form of the particular; the One wears the drag of the many... The 'benefit' of nonduality is ending the tyranny of egoic illusion and awakening to the truth. The 'benefit' of Judaism [or your religion(s)] is responding to that truth with acts of love and devotion...into a culture, community, and ethical tradition; and naming it as God. [27] *(p.4)*

Imagine our relationships with each other if we truly saw God in everyone else and if everyone else saw God in us? Would we hurt or harm each other? What would our relationships be like if we understood our own internal states and those of others, separate from ours, but part of a shared, collective field?

The ability to see the world through another's perspective and to allow them to see yours, to hold more than one worldview at a time, to meet another in a shared sphere of thought is the development of *intersubjective* understanding - a feature of the integral worldview. Our capacity for intersubjectivity emerges from our evolving growth and maturity as adults who continue to learn and grow. Like Erikson's psycho-social stages of development, an intersubjective understanding includes and transcends prior "orders of consciousness," a term coined by Robert Kegan, an American developmental psychologist who argued that cognitive learning continues into adulthood.

In our Interspiritual Age, the experience of nonduality and evolutionary spirituality along with intersubjective understanding allows us to find new meaning in religion and in our relationship with others. Developing our capacity for intersubjective understanding becomes critical for healing collective trauma to "bring your tribe" to "belong to the world." (More on this in Part 2.) For now, the following essay explores intersubjectivity through a fictional character.

④
MULTIPLE BELONGING

How many literary characters can you name who embrace three religions at one time? As a religion teacher who values exposing students to different faith traditions, it was a joy to show my students the film *Life of Pi,* whose main character is a Hindu-Christian-Muslim. The film shines light on the convergence of faith, story, and life - on and off the screen. It asks us to choose between two stories to explain Pi's survival at sea - the animal story representing faith or the human story representing reason. We are not asked which story is True or False, Right or Wrong, but which do we prefer?

In his wish to love God, Pi finds meaning in three different religions at once. His multi-religious practice helps him survive, along with life lessons from his anti-religious zookeeper father, when lost at sea with a Bengal tiger. Pi demonstrates *intersubjectivity* - the ability to hold and value more than one worldview at a time. In asking which story we *prefer* to explain Pi's survival -faith in the fantasy of surviving with a Bengal tiger or reason based on the reality of brutal murder- we bypass the command to believe what an authority figure, a parent, pope, or president, tells us. Like Pi, we choose. And we can choose *more than one.*

While Pi's progressive father prefers his son not flirt with three religions let alone one, he asks only that his son use reason when choosing a path. Pi does-and even adds Jewish mysticism as an adult. While respectfully recognizing the role of doubt, Pi's choice is ultimately based on aesthetic judgement. Thus, he trumps blind faith, making his decision to belong to more than one religion seem rational. Along the way, we learn a little about Hinduism and its multiple Gods, Christianity and its sacrificial Son, and Islam and its submission to Allah. Such education provides us with more color, more perspective, and more opportunities for enriching our own stories, for better or for worse, to guide us in our personal journey through the ocean of life.

Walking away from the film without choosing a story is not an option. This reminds me of a story I once read about a Holocaust survivor. When asked, "After the horrible things you've been through, how can you believe in God?" the survivor replied, "How can I not." Stories help. But we need to be as aware of the stories we tell ourselves as Pi was of his stories. For this reason, interfaith education is critical. Honoring the voices and experiences of individuals and families who choose multiple belonging can be beneficial.

Pioneers from the Jewish community bringing us to the Interspiritual Age where multiple belonging is a norm include: Rabbi Rami Shapiro, author and cofounder of the *Big I Conference on Inclusive Theology, Spirituality and Consciousness,* Mirabai Starr, interspiritual author and teacher, author Ruth Broyd Sharone and producer of *Interfaith The Musical,* and Susan Katz Miller, Jewish and Christian author of *Being Both*. Their work responds to the pressure to evolve. Miller's work, in particular, points to the value that intermarried families bring to interfaith education.

In *Being Both: Embracing Two Religions in One Interfaith Family,* Miller shares how and why some intermarried families raise their children with two religions. *Being Both* is a history lesson and a harbinger. With stories and statistics from surveys of Jewish-Christian families in four different interfaith communities across the country, Miller defuses objections posed by skeptics, such as the argument that the kids will be confused. Her rebuttal, based on interviews with the adult children, parents, clergy, and the teachers in these communities, shows that interfaith kids are *not* confused. Rather, they have wisdom beyond a single faith perspective with positive experiences from their interfaith education.

As the founder of a Jewish-Interfaith congregation, my experience both resembles and differs from Miller's. Rather than teach two religions, I taught one "home" religion-with-an-interfaith orientation. I also noticed that offspring of interfaith families have a propensity for peacemaking and social justice. As Miller reveals, many interfaith kids choose careers that tap their comfort with conflict resolution.

I welcomed the addition of an interfaith teacher's perspective in Miller's survey since the voices of interfaith educators are, for the most part, rejected in religious educational forums. In 2014, at the *"360 Education Models in a Non-360° World"* conference sponsored by the School of Social Works' Jewish Communal Leadership Program at The University of Michigan, I noticed how Jewish interfaith education was not only intentionally excluded but, when offered, dismissed with contempt. This dismissal by leaders of established Jewish schools continues to this day. Interfaith studies remain absent from mainstream religious schools. Yet, the need for solidarity among religionists in the face of *nationalism* may unlock the door to interfaith awareness and interspiritual experience.

I once curated a virtual conference for Jewish-Interfaith Sunday School students to interact with Muslim eighth graders in Jakarta, Indonesia. At the time, interfaith marriage was very rare in Indonesia. The students in Jakarta could not fathom that my students' parents came from different religions and ethnicities. When intermarriage rates began to rise in the capital of Jakarta, the Muslim clerics there expressed concern. In 2023, Indonesia's Supreme Court made it harder for interfaith couples to have their marriages recognized. But, if clerics of all religions were aware of religious education models that preserve and respect their tradition(s) while being open to learning from and sharing the wisdom of all, would they still object?

Miller's release of *The Interfaith Toolkit* with co-author Dalia El Ariny, a student of anthropology of religion who identifies as Italian Egyptian Catholic-Muslim, documents the grassroots movement in the field of interfaith education. As more children grow up holding complex and fluid religious identities, it is even more important, they argue, for researchers to recognize how interfaith organizations can benefit from the experience of interfaith families, and vice versa. Too often, interfaith organizations doing interfaith activism ignore the contributions of interfaith families or teachers experimenting with interfaith education for bridge-building and social justice work. Miller's toolkit is designed to facilitate such conversations which are increasing as our society recognizes the need for *religious literacy*, a form of interfaith education.

As religious nationalism rises, the need for religious literacy becomes more apparent. In their 2025 working report, *Mapping the Field of K-12 Religious Literacy Education,* authors Kate Soules and Dan del Nido write,

"It is clear that the entanglements between religion and public education, which seemed fairly settled even just a decade ago, are increasing, and religious literacy education is needed more than ever." (pp. 49-50)

Since public school districts could become financially incentivized to adopt curricula that favors Christianity -*not as one of many religions about which to learn but as the only religion students are expected to follow*- the need for religious literacy and interfaith education in our *religious* schools may be critical. Ironically, religious school might be the last institution shielded from government mandates indoctrinating students with religious nationalism. Jewish and other religious communities may find solidarity in teaching their "home" religions within an interfaith orientation, or a similar model. In the meantime, we can support public schools advancing religious literacy while knowing non-public students may be missing out. The chart below accentuates those involved in advancing religious literacy in education, a topic deserving its own book.

⑤
IF YOU MEET A RELIGIOUS LEADER ON THE ROAD [28]

If you meet a religious leader on the road... *and* you ask if they include interfaith or interspiritual education in their religious school programs, they'll laugh at best and threaten you at worse. At least, that's been my experience.

When I led *Jewbilation*, a congregation for intermarried Jewish families at a time when interfaith families were not welcome in mainstream Jewish institutions (which was why I created it), a group of local rabbis met to discuss 'me'. Apparently, I was a threat. It is still painful to remember the phone call from the then-president of the JCC (Jewish Community Center) disinviting me from an event for all members of the Jewish community to learn about the local, educational Jewish programs available to them despite my reputation as a stellar Hebrew school teacher.

At the time, these Jewish community leaders were uncomfortable with the way I included universal spiritual truths from other traditions in my sermons let alone in my religious school classroom. So, I was further marginalized. But that is where growth happens - on the edge. I continued experimenting with interfaith belonging. But I also understood these rabbis' concerns. Understanding their fears allowed me to address them.

For established leaders, including interfaith curricula to strengthen faith formation was counterintuitive. These leaders, clergy, and school principals, kept it far away while paying lip service. Typical responses to the idea of interfaith education included the following:

1. If I teach other faiths to my students, **they won't have faith/follow** the religion assigned to them by parents, communities, blood, or state.

2. If I teach other faiths to my students, **they won't identify** with the religion assigned to them.

3. If I teach other faiths to my students, **there won't be time** to teach the one assigned to them.

In my experience, these are fears, not reasons. Let's take a closer look.

SCENARIO 1. *Interfaith education will weaken a child's faith.* Let me refute this argument with a story.

I once attended a Jewish worship service where a stranger was present. In the middle of the service, he was introduced as an Arab Muslim from Israel. He shared that his ability to attend *and enjoy* a Jewish service was because he felt secure in his own faith. Of course, he was an adult so there was less concern about joining another service when his faith had already formed. But he was there to talk about a successful program in Israel where Muslim and Jewish *children* learned Arabic and Hebrew side by side and experienced familiarity with each other's religions. He promoted children of different faiths learning alongside each other. It was the only school of its kind at the time and sadly there are not many more today.

The real fear is *not* that interfaith will weaken *existing* faith, but that faith is weak to begin with and needs strengthening *before* "other" ideas are introduced. That sounds like fear.[29] *Where is this fear coming from?*

It comes from a worldview in which we must all express loyalty to our tribes for the sake of survival. This story worked at certain times in our evolution. It no longer reflects the cusp from which the evolution of human culture now lurches. Today's youth can benefit from an education that teaches a world-centric or cosmos-centric worldview where multiple belonging, without sacrificing the integrity of each religion, is a norm.

Keeping religious literacy or interfaith awareness out of the public and/or private religious school classrooms impairs the ability of future generations to solve global problems in a multi-faith world. It shows a lack of respect for interfaith awareness and religious literacy. This can lead to ignorance and discrimination against others. In fact, the high level of religious illiteracy in this country keeps us from learning about religions and overcoming religious conflict.[30] It prevents the understanding that arises from interfaith learning.

SCENARIO 2. *Teaching other religions alongside your own tradition results in a child converting to or identifying with another religion.* To this argument, I have three responses:

1st. Unless a child finds a *family* they like better than theirs and that family practices another religion, why worry. If they like another religion, that's great. It shows interest in learning about spirituality. I found ways to enrich my students' understanding of Judaism through teaching about and appreciating beliefs and practices of other religions without diminishing their connection to Judaism. Interfaith education is an opportunity to learn what religions have in common *and* what's unique about each.

2nd. If a child is attracted to another religion and wants to explore it, assist rather than resist. As a child, I was drawn to Native American spirituality and Eastern philosophy. *What if adults had encouraged my exposure to these traditions when I was young?* I might have felt a trust among people of different traditions willing to share teachings and wisdom, and in turn share mine. Instead, I felt wisdom was kept from me.

In 2012, when I attended the first interfaith conference for educators, we were asked to put our fears on the table. Many participants said they were afraid their children would identify with a different religion. I understand that fear. I saw it with my parents when I married out of our tribe. We see it in the way Tevya *(Fiddler on the Roof)* responds to his third daughter, Chava, as she falls in love with a Russian, not a Jew. But holding back from sharing the teachings of other faith traditions is not justified. As teachers, we can use our students' interest to guide them in their spiritual growth. As parents, we can develop a trusting relationship with our children when we approach their interests with respect. *Isn't that what faith development (and good parenting) is about?*

3rd. The dominant ethno-centric worldview that has served our tribes well may no longer be *evolutionary* appropriate. The purpose of religious identification - protection, survival, continuity, preservation from 'other' tribes - no longer drives affiliation. Our values are changing. Religious identity without interfaith experience holds back the next generation from participating in the emergence of values that lead to a greater good for all religions and their tribes. We ought to assist it, not block it.

SCENARIO 3. *There's no time to teach interfaith.*

It is true that competing extracurricular activities impinge on after-school religious programs. Institutions that educate youth in religion are already limited in time for instruction. But that does not mean an interfaith education is out of the question. If we *value* something, we make time. To exclude interfaith education in a religious school program because "there is no time" is a polite excuse for a lack of interest or a cover up of fear.

Administrators could support teachers in innovating with ways to teach interfaith. Learning a religion(s) and exposure to interfaith can go hand in hand. Material which cannot be taught in the allotted time and does not require face to face learning, as interfaith often does, can be learned in other ways, at other times. The "flipped classroom" model is one example. In congregational afterschool programs where many students also participate in religious youth groups, there are opportunities for bringing an interspiritual approach to teaching. Now is the time for religious educators to innovate with interfaith education in their lessons. Certainly, virtual lessons and AI will be contributing to new ways of teaching. Integrating interfaith literacy in religious school classrooms is the future of religious education in the Interspiritual Age.

Underlying these three scenarios is also a fear that is not expressed by clergy and educators because they themselves may be unaware of it. The unhealed, unresolved, unconscious collective traumas that belong to our ancestors, but which are held in our bodies can also be behind the fear of introducing anything different. Such fear leads to a distrust of learning about others let alone with them.

Such distrust keeps us believing that our safety lies in our isolation when in fact what we need is to develop trust and come together in solidarity.

How can religious leaders overcome the fears that get in the way?

1. *Inhabit an open mind.* Learn what interfaith education looks like. Meet with those doing it or read about their experiences.[31]

2. *Adopt a long view.* Anticipate new models of religion education adapting to our changing world. Design lessons to support it.

3. *Pilot an interfaith or interspiritual program.* Test it in your school. Start with one teacher and class. Invest in success, not failure.

4. *Offer workshops for healing intergenerational trauma.* Narrative therapy may be inadequate to address unhealed collective trauma. Somatic therapy, tapping, EMDR, and other modes of embodied healing are now used to heal unhealed collective, intergenerational, historical, and cultural trauma.

Today, religious leaders are more open to sharing wisdom from other traditions. Perhaps they are ready to leave their fears on the side of the road behind them and follow it to the Interspiritual Age.

⑥
HOW DOES EUROPE DO IT?

What can we learn from how people in other countries teach religion? In a world of changing conditions and demographics, academic and professional practitioners who are members of the Religion Education Association (REA), seek to improve RE (religion education) curricula with evidence-based research. In 2016, I attended an REA conference where I met RE teachers from around the world including Belgium, Germany, Austria, England, Spain, Turkey, Nigeria, Canada, Israel, Australia, and the United States. Since then, I continue to learn about the bigger world of RE. Notably, unlike in the United States, RE is a required class in Europe's high schools.

In England, all students are required to study RE until age 18. They learn religion in multi-faith classrooms. But RE teachers are not as prepared as they can be when the curriculum does not keep up with changing demographics. *"We think non-believers and those with informal beliefs need to be treated more seriously as a growing part of the picture,"* said one RE teacher. Another called the program out of date saying teachers needed better training across Europe.[32]

The effect of changing demographics on Europe's *Catholic* schools resulted in many Belgian Muslim immigrants choosing to send their children to Catholic schools instead of public schools. (Both are financed by the State. The former is organized by a board but created by a religious order.) At the time, religion taught in Catholic schools was treated with more respect than in public schools where *"[RE] requirements are [were] ignored, or watered down."* I was told many parents preferred their children to learn a different religion in a school that respects religion than to learn their family's religion in a school that does not. According to a Belgian professor at the time, 80% of students at her Catholic school in Brussels were Muslim.

Germany and Austria teach RE differently from Europe. Their students learn religion with "same faith" peers. Bernhard Gruemme, Faculty of Catholic Theology at Ruhr Universität Bochum, explained that in these two countries students do not learn religion in a multi-faith setting. Instead, they learn one religion from teachers trained to teach it to those students affiliated with it. This assumes there are religion teachers for each religion represented by the students in each school.

What if there is no teacher for one's religion? What if students do not affiliate with any religion? In these cases, said Bernhard, a student must take philosophy. Interestingly, integral philosophers suggest the exclusion of philosophy from the study of religion contributes to increased political polarization today.[33] Could the integration of philosophy and religion give us the skills to think critically and to form thoughtful, meaningful identities and relationships with others?[34]

Separating reason and faith can sink our ability to understand different worldviews and to express beliefs not as facts but as ways of seeing and making meaning. If we can do that, surely, we can come together for our common, higher Good. Imagine my surprise and delight when I visited a poster session devoted to Philosophy in the RE Classroom. The presenter cited Matthew Lipman, founder of the *Institute for the Advancement of Philosophy for Children* (IAPC),[35] with whom I personally studied 40 years ago. (To see his program prosper in Belgium while it got little traction in the US reminded me of Sugarman's music - a cultural phenomenon in S. Africa that was buried in the U.S.) If Europe can borrow *Philosophy for Children* from America, then we can borrow RE from Europe. I believe we can learn from the experiences of Europe's teachers and improve upon it by teaching all religions *and* philosophy. Afterall, Einstein said science without religion is lame and religion without science is blind. Why not teach both - reason and faith- in the religious school classroom.

⑦
GLOBAL CITIZENS DO IT

To understand the interspiritual worldview where the self is experienced as interdependent and interconnected in relation to others, we can ask, *what does it mean to identify with eight billion people on the planet?* Then we can learn about Garry Davis.

The Legacy of Garry Davis[36]

When Garry Davis, a young Broadway actor in 1941 -an understudy for Danny Kaye in a Cole Porter musical about US Army inductees- entered World War II, it would change his life. His older brother was killed while fighting in Europe and Garry enlisted. He flew bombing missions over Germany, but he could not bear the realization that he was helping kill other people just as his beloved brother had been killed. "I felt humiliated that I was part of it," he later said. In 1948, he declared himself a citizen of the world, and refused to be part of an idea that people must have national citizenship when nations resort to violence, hatred, and war. He gave up his US citizenship and turned in his passport in Paris, which made him no longer legally welcome in France or anywhere else on planet Earth.

Without a home, Garry set up a personal living space in a tiny spot of land where the United Nations was meeting, and which France had temporarily declared open to the world. Calling the UN's bluff, he declared that as a citizen of the world this spot of land must be his home. This created an international incident and world fame.

Living on the street or a makeshift tent, first at the UN conference in Paris and then by a river separating France from Germany, Garry succeeded in calling attention to his cause and gathering support from public figures like Jean-Paul Sartre, Simone de Beauvoir, Albert Camus, Andre Breton and Andre Gide. He was cheered by a crowd of 20,000 young protestors and cited for his work by Albert Einstein and Eleanor Roosevelt.

He started an organization devoted to world citizenship, the *World Government of World Citizens*, to issue passports and advocate for peace around the world. Garry Davis seized a moment, insisting the UN live up to its words about global peacemaking, and ultimately using its Universal Declaration of Human Rights as the foundation for his enduring organization. (We can get all get world passports.)

The notion of global citizenship is powerful. *We are all citizens of the world,* and it is up to us to choose a future of shared humanity and shared prosperity over hatred and violence. It took the courage of Garry Davis to take an incredible personal risk by giving up his own national citizenship in Paris in 1948, without a clear idea of what he would do next. A song-and-dance man and ex-GI became a hero and an example for others.

Garry gave hope to refugees around the world who yearn for relief and the justice of global citizenship which could save their lives by giving them and all of us a place to belong - our world. He once said, *"I am not a man without a country, merely a man without a nationality."*[37]

Who is a Global Citizen?

University of Michigan psychology professor Fiona Lee pointed to Carlos Ghosn, former CEO of Nissan as a model global citizen. Although he has since fallen out of favor, he was so adored by the Japanese people in whose country he once resided that they named a Bento box after him. He helped companies turn around financially and improved their economies. Many Japanese wanted him to run for office. The experience of an outsider in a country with low historical migration adapting to Japanese culture and being revered by its people may not seem strange today but Lee looked for deeper answers.

In her research, she identified CQ - cultural adaptability, cultural intelligence, and curiosity as keys to global citizenry. Ghosn, who grew up in multiple countries (Brazil, Lebanon, and France) with high rates of historical migration — a sign that immigrants are welcome — and who spoke four languages, had high cultural adaptability and intelligence. His background helped him develop a cross-cultural management style emphasizing diversity as a core business asset. "You learn from diversity," he said, "but you're comforted by commonality."

For Lee, global citizens come in two types: those who want to help the world and those who easily travel or work outside their home' country or who often connect to others around the planet. These two types can overlap. However, we must ask: *If global citizenship requires traveling and working abroad, won't this result in an elitist group reaping the benefits of global exposure?*

Lee's study showed that living abroad was neither necessary nor sufficient for improving one's cultural adaptability, a key trait of global citizenship. Her results showed that study abroad students who live with host families, learn the language, and befriend locals increase their cultural adaptability. Those who don't, maintain or lower their cultural adaptability. What is not so obvious is that study abroad students who do not adapt to the culture score *lower* on cultural adaptability *than students who do not study abroad.* In other words, one can develop cultural adaptability and increase global exposure without ever leaving home. How?

The work of Parag Khanna, a geopolitical expert, offers insights. Khanna found that global citizens "often connect to others around the planet" (the second type of global citizen). They see themselves in terms of 'connectivity' vs sovereignty.[38] For this type of global citizen, relationships are more 'horizontal' than vertical, more egalitarian than hierarchical, and increasingly digital. Thus, there are global citizens who easily travel or work abroad. There are also those who easily connect with others around the globe without ever leaving home.

The Helpful Global Citizen

The type of global citizen *"who wants to help others"* is part of a growing evolutionary impulse. We see it in the number of people who join sponsorship circles to welcome and resettle refugees. Helping others everywhere is in everyone's interest. Cultural adaptability, intelligence, and connectivity are indicators of some of the global citizenship skills we need today. *What other skills can we nurture to be wise and compassionate global citizens?*

Helping others across different cultures requires deep listening and understanding of others' beliefs and ideas, including in the domain of religion. Author Doug Johnston argues in his book, *Religion, The Missing Dimension of Statecraft*, that the failure of American diplomats to understand the role of religion in other cultures has impeded peace making around the world. Understanding other people's relationships to religion (at home and abroad) is part of global citizenship. This kind of learning, along with a world-centric worldview, is more likely to develop in the religious congregation that encourages interfaith education than the one that does not. Interestingly, the impulse to help others appears stronger among those identifying as global versus national citizens.[39]

Global Citizens and Religious Education (RE)

In The Interspiritual Classroom (TIC) that I developed over years of teaching students from interfaith families, we toured different houses of worship and participated in different worship services. We welcomed guest teachers from other religions, visited classrooms of peers in other afterschool religious programs, and communicated through blogs or video calls with students in other countries to learn about their communities, faiths, and identities. And we gave them an opportunity to learn about us. We did all of this without leaving "home".

While the interspiritual worldview values interdependence, connecting with all people, with our global community, it's important to remember that the development of an interdependent self is not a replacement for the way self is valued in other worldviews. It is a new value that integrates with prior views of self-development. It is part of our evolution of self in relation to others. When we integrate other ideas of self into a new idea, we bring what is valuable about those other ways of being. This includes what is valuable dependency, one who depends on family which is typical of the traditional worldview, what is valuable about independence, self-reliance which characterizes the modern worldview, as well as what is valuable about being one's authentic, self-realized self, a feature of the postmodern or progressive worldview.

All these experiences of self are integrated in the interdependent self that marks the integral worldview. The interspiritual-minded teacher teaches the home religion in different ways, dependently on the authority of its traditions, independently as it opens to reform, authentically as it finds a balance between tradition and renewal, and interdependently as it allows students to learn from other religions and share theirs.

The interspiritual-minded teacher can enhance their students' religious understanding by juxtaposing the home religion's lessons with spiritual teachings of other traditions. An interspiritual-minded teacher can help students recognize the values of each worldview while teaching what is valuable about the interspiritual worldview. This teacher can help students develop their spiritual intelligence with skills identified by author Cindy Wiggleworth in *SQ21: The 21 Skills of Spiritual Intelligence*.

The skills of spiritual intelligence, says Wiggleworth, help us grow from ego-centric behavior into a more loving, empathic, and peaceful higher self. These latter qualities are needed to become wise, compassionate human beings, which is what we need now to join as interdependent world citizens capable of solving our global problems. As we create new forms for the Interspiritual Age, we build movements bold enough to embrace our shared humanity. Our classrooms can be conduits for opening minds to a new worldview and encouraging young people to become helpful global citizens who belong in and to the World.

Born to be Kind

I am reminded of a story about a young college student who wrote a letter in 1961 to the Rebbe (the orthodox Rabbi Menachem Mendel Schneerson, leader of the Chabad-Lubavitcher movement). The student shared his despondency over the world leading him to suicidal ideation. The Rebbe pushed back. He told the student that this whole letter was full of his own expectations and disappointments, as if everybody owes him everything but...it did not occur to him, said the Rebbe, that he might owe something to society. The Rebbe offered this troubled student something more powerful than sympathy -a solution. Instead of brooding over his problems, the Rebbe redirected his focus. He told the depressed young man that he must get away from himself, and begin to think of others...to give, and to give generously. *"The opportunities are many and the need is great."*

The student took the Rebbe's advice to heart and went on to lead a productive, full and meaningful life. He became a professor of religion and helped other students find their own life purposes.

Although this story refers to a different period in history, similarities exist. We need to think more communally. Not just at a national level, politically, but a global one. Not just at a tribal level, religiously, but a universal one.

⑧
GROWING WITH GOD

I tried not to say it. I tried to use a synonym to avoid uttering the one word that might cause my student's grandfather to walk out of the High Holiday service I was leading. I failed.

As soon as I said GOD, Bob (z'l) stood up and walked out. While his behavior was not new to my student and his family, it was to me. Bob did not believe in God. He had reasons that were rational and a story that was personal. He could not tolerate The Name. I learned that I cannot assume to know what God means to others, and that I needed to investigate further what God meant to me. *Who/What is God?*

My beliefs about God had changed over time. I believed in God as a child because I was told to. This God was outside of me. When JFK died, I looked into the night sky and believed he was with God. Up there. Far away and still near. Then I thought God was in things, like nature, down here. When our dog was lost, I asked God for help through a rock. I trusted God would intervene. (Lo and behold, I found our dog.) When God didn't fix our family's problems, I lost faith. How could God let bad things happen *to* me, my family, my tribe, and others? Since God forgot me, I forgot God. But not really, as this memory shows:

When I signed up to live and work on a religious kibbutz in the state of Israel, bad things had not yet happened to my family. By the time I arrived, they had. With no moorings, I sat in my dorm room smoking a non-filtered cigarette...on Shabbat. I was rebelling as I outgrew the childhood concept of "an old, white-bearded man in the sky watching over me." (Actually, my image of God was a young man in a tuxedo, bigger than the universe and with a wispy tail flying around the earth. I drew Him in pencil on lined paper.)

As my lifelong yearning for spirituality got louder, I looked around. Soon, I was studying a form of Hinduism based on *Advaita*

Vedanta (nondual) philosophy, chanted daily from the *Bhagavad Gita,* waved Arati lights, read the *Mahabharata,* learned meditation and yoga, cooked and ate in a Guru-led spiritual community, and co-led its weekly children's program. The image for my Hindu period is this:

I am sitting on a cushion in a large hall full of people, all of whom are also sitting on cushions, draped in wool prayer shawls, as we chant a mantra and meditate. The Guru glides through the hall, brushing us with a giant peacock feather to initiate the spiritual transmission of energy from realized teacher to student, aka Shaktipat, an uncoiling of energy at the base of the spine that shoots to the crown.

Through many ashram retreats, I learned about God as knower and known, seer and seen, consciousness beyond the limitations of this world. In *God is Everything: The Radical Path of Nondual Judaism,* Rabbi and scholar Jay Michaelson explains Vedanta through the words of Vivekananda, *"You, as body, mind, or soul, are a dream, but what you really are, is Existence, Knowledge, Bliss. You are the God of this universe. You are creating the whole universe and drawing it in."* (p. 80) In other words, we are all God. There is no separation.

According to Vedanta, we long for nondual experience because when we feel separated from God, we know it's not natural. It's not natural because it's an illusion. But, says Rupert Spira, thinking it's real, *"The separate self or ego is prone to vulnerability and insecurity and thus seeks to defend itself.... inclined to feel unconfident, inferior and unloved...it seeks to aggrandize itself...it seeks fulfillment through the acquisition of objects, substances, activities, states of mind or relationships..."* Like Buddhism, it is the *attachment* to things that causes suffering.

The nondual philosophy of Vedanta inspired me on my spiritual journey but the Hindu community I joined was not sustainable. I came down from the proverbial mountaintop to apply its lessons in the world. It is one thing to become one with God in a universe that is illusory (acosmism) and another to be devoted to God in a universe that is a manifestation of God. In other words, as Jay Michaelson notes in Vivekananda's *Gospel of Ramakrishna,* if you're a devotee in the world and not on the mountaintop, then what you want is to eat sugar, not to become sugar. (*God is Everything*, p. 134) While becoming sugar was tempting, I ultimately chose to eat it.

A dream came next. In the dream, I hovered over a Torah service, all in Hebrew, not my native tongue. This led me to visit a friend in Jerusalem. There, in the dark of night, I spoke silently, from my heart to God. *"God, why aren't You with me?"* I did not expect an answer let alone one before I finished the question. *"Why aren't you with Me?"* (The emphasis was on different words.) I felt an electric charge and an invitation to rediscover my Jewish roots. The irony, of course, is that the answer revealed the fallacy of the question. God is always with us. Having found mysticism in Hinduism, I trusted I'd find it in Judaism. I joined a Hasidic study group.

In an all-women's Hasidic study group, I could not get enough of Judaism's mystical teachings, or *Kabbalah*. Torah came alive with layers of interpretation and meaningful engagement with the text. Soon, I wrote my own *midrashim* (interpretations) and I devoted time to learning how to chant verses of Torah. Thus, in the Jewish Hasidic movement founded by the Ba'al Shem Tov (1698-1760), I found nondual Judaism. Eventually, I left Hasidism. Its treatment of women, disdain for gentiles, lack of interest in non-Jewish teachings, sense of superiority in the Jewish community, and condemnation of interfaith marriage kept me feeling left out, despite neo-Hasidic claims of Oneness.

In Hinduism, the insistence that life is an illusion hits you on the head from the get-go. In Judaism, nondualism must be pulled out. God is both near and far, imminent and transcendent. Rabbi Rami Shapiro cites the book of Isaiah to describe this experience. *"Peace, peace to the one who is far and the one who is near."* (57:19) In his book, *Zen Mind, Jewish Mind*, Shapiro explains the verse as follows, *"The 'one who is far' experiences God as transcendent. The 'one who is near' experiences God as immanent. Both seekers, having found God, will find peace, but not the same peace. The peace of the first is experienced as awe. The peace of the second is experienced as love. A complete peace...comes only to those who experience the nondual Divine that embraces both far and near. Their peace is the blending of awe and love."* (p. 70)

It was validating to find a nondual path of Judaism also found in other religions and usually referred to as mysticism. In the Interspiritual Age, the nondualism of religions are appreciated for their similarities and differences. It's worth noting Michaelson's take on Judaism's approach to nondualism. Jewish sources, he says, usually depict nonduality from the top down –beginning with an infinite God and moving to the consequences– rather than bottom up, deriving insights from experience and then working our way 'up' from there. Says Michaelson,

> *To start with God is to start from an unproven, uncertain, and highly debatable premise...the word 'God' carries...all sorts of associations that have nothing to do with the nondual view: a character who acts in history, for example, or has some special reaction to prayer or ethics or ritual.*

Fast forward back to Bob. It is my suspicion that the Jewish pedagogy in Bob's upbringing turned him off. What if he learned about God from the bottom up rather than the top down? Would his experience have been different?

Long before Bob, I knew religious liturgy and pedagogy left many people feeling excluded. Me, too. No wonder so many of my peers left Judaism and many others left religion altogether. In *Zen Mind, Jewish Mind*, Rabbi Rami Shapiro writes, *"I haven't prayed in synagogue in years. I find the liturgy too wordy, the service too long, and the need to translate the dualism inherent in the prayers into the nondualism of my experience too exhausting."* (p. 95) We could all benefit from revisions to our liturgy by allowing them to speak to people with different experiences.

How we innovate with prayer, however, requires care. Rabbi Rami Efal advised me not to go too far with changing the words of prayers to suit modern sensibilities. In doing so, he said, we would be playing with the "erasure of our ancestors." Thus, new versions of Jewish liturgy are often presented as optional additions, not replacements. However, we can honor both dual and nondual experiences of God. In an interview with Daniel Epstein, creator of *Portraits in Faith*, Rabbi Tirzah Firestone speaks to the meaning she finds in a sacred "I-Thou" relationship with God (a dualist model) while also recognizing and knowing that everything is One/*Echad*, that nothing is not Spirit. Her memoir, *With Roots in Heaven*, is a testimony to the consequences she drew from her spiritual journey.

Having a different concept of God as an adolescent might not have prevented my parents' divorce or stopped someone from setting off a bomb in my family's mailbox because my brother was gay. These events nudged me into finding new ways to relate to God and helped me better handle future challenges. And so, as we honor our ancestors by including their versions of praying to a dualist's concept of God, we must also prepare for our descendants. From an evolutionary perspective, the future has a voice. The future is interspiritual and a nondual experience of God is also part of it.

My brief review of different concepts and experiences of God mirrors the collective. According to Jay Michaelson, Rabbi Zalman Shachter-Shalomi claimed, *"We have moved past the stage of deism which he associates with Ein Aroch (there is no measurement to God) and even past theism (Ein Zulatecha, there is no God besides You) and into monism (Efes Blitecha, there is nothing besides You.)"* (p. 138) As we evolve, so does God.

In *Zen Mind, Jewish Mind*, Rabbi Rami Shapiro explains, *"When the prophet Malachi hears YHVH say, 'I am YHVH, I do not change,' we should understand YHVH to be saying, 'I am YHVH. I do not change because I am change."* (p. 69) As God changes, so do we.

We can grow with God into our next evolutionary stage, the Interspiritual Age, by welcoming different theologies of God within our traditions and alongside those of other religions and let them speak to each other.

I am fond of a Jewish story told by Rabbi Nisson Dovid Dubov that demonstrates the different focus of Jews in their understanding of God. Before Jonathan Sacks became Chief Rabbi of the UK, he studied at a Chassidic yeshiva in a Chassidic village in Israel. In the middle of his studies, his Chassidic study partner said to him, *"The difference between me and you is you think about G-d all day and I think about myself all day!"* The Chief Rabbi was surprised. He assumed his study partner, born in an isolated *religious* village and spoon fed with faith and stories of the righteous would be thinking about God all day, and that he, who was educated in the halls of secular philosophy, would be thinking of himself all day. The student said to Sacks, *"You failed to understand my point. You who attended university and received a degree in philosophy know that you exist; your only question is whether G-d exists, so you think about G-d all day. I, who was raised in the Chassidic village know there is a G-d, but my whole question is where I fit into the picture to fulfill God's will. So, I think about myself all day!"*

In contrast, it was a Buddhist American Sikh who brought to my awareness the obvious God crisis among Jews. In her experience as a therapist working with American Jews, we had lost our trust in God. For religious Israeli Jews, it may be that they lost their trust in Man, too. Referring to the story above, Rabbi Dubov elaborates that from God's perspective, God exists and we are infinitesimally small manifestations of the Divine creative energy. From our perspective, we and our world exist—the whole question is how God fits into our world. That world includes many religions. Each one contains wisdom we can learn from each other. In listening, we learn and grow, with God, and with others, through dual and nondual theologies, through religious and interspiritual themes. The next time I was to lead a High Holiday service, I would be prepared.

(9)
A NEW-FANGLED PREACHER TEACHER [40]

In a world undergoing a paradigm shift in cultural consciousness, we each experience movement towards the Interspiritual Age in unique ways. The following essay is a review of my personal spiritual journey to dater.

The 18th century Rabbi Zusya of Anapoli said he feared that when he died, the angels would ask him not *"Why weren't you more like Moses?"* but *"Why weren't you more like Zusya?"*

How do we become *ourselves* (and not who parents, principals, preachers, or presidents tell us to be) in this changing world? Contemporary Quaker educator and writer, Parker Palmer, gave this advice:

"Before I can tell my life what I want to do with it, I must listen to my life telling me who I am."

I listened. "Teach!" said my life. **"Not just Faith. Philosophy!"**

"Okay!" I said. And went about preparing myself.

I trained with Professor Matthew Lipman, the founder of Philosophy for Children, inspired by his belief that young people could think critically, carefully, and creatively, and make reasonable judgments about what to do or believe.

Life responded. A synagogue's religious school director agreed to let me teach ethics to 4th graders — if I taught Hebrew and Jewish history, too. It was a deal that lasted three years with the same class. I taught Judaism to Jewish kids — yet we also engaged in thinking philosophically.

Still, I hadn't fulfilled my promise. I wondered how, with interfaith marriage on the rise, I could prepare my students (and my own children) for a world quite different from the one I inherited. What would they need to know to survive and thrive in an increasingly multi-faith society?

"Before I can tell my life what I want to do with it, I must listen to my life, telling me who I am."

I listened. "Teach!" said my life. **"Not just One Faith. Multiple faiths!"**

I trained with Rabbi Joseph Gelberman at All Faiths Seminary in NYC, inspired by his motto, *"Never instead of, always in addition to."* I was ordained as an Interfaith Minister, completed the coursework of his Rabbinic Seminary International's Modern Rabbi program, and accomplished an Adult Bat Mitzvah!

Life responded again. I founded *Jewbilation: Jewish Roots with Interfaith Wings,* a congregation for religiously unaffiliated families and led it for six years. The school that came out of it was a deal that lasted 15 years with the same group of children. I taught them to connect with their Jewish roots AND with the rich heritage of the world's major religious traditions.

We studied the stories of the Torah AND the parables of the New Testament. We practiced Jewish holidays AND learned about their relationship to the holidays of other faiths. We visited Jewish synagogues and temples AND non-Jewish churches, mosques, and gurdwaras.

We watched movies, like *Fiddler on the Roof* AND *Whale Rider;* we saw Tevya (the Jewish peddler) and Koro (the Māori chief) confront the same, ever-familiar, perennial problem: How to maintain one's traditions in the face of great and rapid societal change?

For their *Interfaith B-Mitzvahs*, my students chanted in Hebrew AND shared a Native American blessing. Or a Mennonite song. Or a Buddhist prayer.

The interfaith couples I married stood under the wedding *chuppah* (Jewish wedding canopy), circled each other 7 times, crushed the glass AND lit Unity Candles. Or exchanged Arras coins, a Latin tradition. Or did *Saptapadi*, the Hindu marriage rite around the fire.

But...

As inter-religious conflict spreads across the globe, being familiar with other faiths was not enough. How could my students connect with the people who practiced them?

"I must listen to my life telling me who I am."

I listened. "Teach!" said my life. **"Not just Many Faiths. Interfaith!"**[41]

So, I introduced my students to inspiring people living sacred lives, people I met at interfaith events sponsored by our local interfaith organization, and I joined the board to design future programs.

Jaspreet welcomed my students to his *Gurdwara,*[42] where his class applied the teachings of the Guru Granth Sahib to their lives, and shared *langar*[43] with us. We drove home that wintery night, our bellies full and our minds enamored with the Sikh religion.

At Chinmaya Mission, Sharada and her staff welcomed my students to a school-wide assembly and invited them to a middle school class on Hindu culture. My students recognized concepts they learned studying Jewish Mussar. In the *prakriti* and *vikrti*[44] of Hinduism, they saw the *yetzer ha-tov* and *yetzer ha-ra*[45] of Judaism. They saw themselves in the Other. And they left beaming, holding *prasad*[46] in their hands and hearts.

Ernestine, a Unity Church minister, co-hosted an Interfaith Passover with me so our students could experience the Seder together. When the *Twelve Powers* of *New Thought* (a spiritual and philosophical movement within Unity) and the *Ten Sefirot*[47] of *Kabbalah* (Jewish mystical tradition) overlapped, all our students lit up. They saw themselves in the Other.

The Tony Blair Faith Foundation allowed my students to "do interfaith" on a global scale. By joining a LIVE video conference with peers at a Muslim School in Jakarta and blogging with Hindu peers at a boarding school in India, all these students shared experiences about faith, identity, and community.

But...

As globalization encroaches on *all* our markers of identity, our young people need a revised foundation story for humanity. Who are we? Why are we here? How can we live in a multi-faith/cultural world together? Can we find ways to honor our religious traditions without "othering"?

Again, I listened. "Lead!" said my life. **"Not just Interfaith. InterSpirituality!"**[48]

Life responded. Like the rabbis of old who designed *Hanukkah* to halt a dangerous nationalistic trend by emphasizing a miracle of light over a military victory, I re-cast this holiday to make room for an experience out of which our individual differences are shared and celebrated. From here we celebrate how our individual tribes appreciate differences and gain inspiration.

As I continue to listen, my life tells me, "Write!" and "Speak!"

Life responds with opportunities to draw on wisdom from *within* my tribe, recognition from *without,* and moments of *reunion* among them all.

I'm not always certain my words hit the mark of my aim, or recover when I stumble, but I am certain of this: When there's no life left to listen to, I will know how to answer the angels who greet me. I will have been myself. I will have been *who I was meant to be.*

"Before we tell our lives what to do, we must listen to our life telling us who we are."

And let us say, *Amen.*

⑩
TIPS FOR BELONGING

Some of us may be reluctant to leave the womb of the tribe to belong to the World, the Interspiritual Age. We need intention *(kavanah)* to dismantle ethno-centrism and reconstruct it within a new world-centric structure. We need courage to integrate our values, religious teachings, and tribes. To hold a container of love and belonging as we do this, I offer several tips.

Tip 1. Relate to Religion Responsibly

We cannot ignore our world's religions. We cannot go around, under, or over them. We cannot bypass them. This only avoids the inevitable, viz., going *through* them. Going through our religions lets us adapt them to the emerging, evolutionarily necessary worldview that is part of human development. How we go through matters. We must do so *responsibly (achrayut)*.

To engage with religion responsibly is to understand how religions affect us, how they affect others, how they affected us and others in the past and how they might affect us and others in the future. It means relating to religions' practitioners with critical thought - asking good questions, engaging in analysis, exercising evaluation, interpretation, reflection, contemplation, discussion, and dialogue. It means learning with an open mind to grow spiritually and with epistemic humility. It means *integrating* the lessons we've learned from ego-centric (individual) and ethno-centric (tribal) consciousness by expanding our values to include world-centric consciousness (universal). We do so with faith, reason, and respectful curiosity.

Taking responsibility for creating a new relationship with religion requires the ability to first step away from the current relationship we have or don't have and look with new eyes. Too often, when we over-identify with religion, we cannot step outside even for a moment. But if we succeed, we see what is before us, how it affects us and others, and whether those consequences are beneficial or harmful. We can ask: Do our spiritual practices and worldly actions result in culture's evolution towards the good? This is a moral question. The phrase, "knowing them by their fruits," is one way of evaluating our spiritual teachings and actions. Do they bring about the intended results? By stepping out of our religion's bubbles, we gain additional perspectives and can take responsibility for our beliefs and behaviors, interspiritually. If beliefs and behaviors fail to yield the fruits that improve our moral development, spread loving-kindness within and among our many different communities, then we may let them go. The very nature of an Interspiritual Age means taking all tribes into account. This responsibility leads to freedom.

Tip 2. Choose Freedom, Choose Well

Jean Paul Sartre, a famous 20th century Existentialist, quipped that *man is condemned to be free.* For, once thrown into the world, each of us is responsible for everything we say and do. Paradoxically, the more for which we are responsible, the more freedom we accrue. How can that be? It depends on our understanding of freedom. We must choose carefully the kind of freedom we value most.

In *The Emancipation of the Mind*, historian Matthew Stewart describes two conflicting theories of freedom - atomic and reflective. They led us, he says, respectively into and out of the Civil War. Stewart explains that the atomic theory of freedom is based on the idea that freedom is for individuals only. As such, individual humans are like distinct atoms in motion *"entirely independent of equality and even inclined to oppose it. Any attempt to make the atoms more equal -to speed some up and slow others down- can only come at the expense of freedom"* [49] for other atoms.

In contrast, the reflective theory of freedom sees humans not as atoms but creatures of consciousness. We reflect! To reflect requires a degree of self-consciousness. Hegel saw self-consciousness as a stage of consciousness in *The Phenomenology of Spirit*. In this stage, consciousness becomes aware of itself as a subject through a struggle for recognition with another self-consciousness. For Hegel, the struggle between master and slave (aka lord and bondsman) reveals how, through a dialectic process, we achieve self-consciousness and thus the possibility to explore identity and freedom. The goal is not to be the master in a master-slave relationship; for the master is not free without the slave to acknowledge the master's dominance. Nor is it better to be a slave who only knows their freedom when they realize they can withhold the recognition the master seeks. To be free, both must recognize the other as worthy of freedom and resolve the tension between them.

As reflective beings, we can look in the proverbial mirror and learn that *"our degree of freedom is in relation to our degree of self-understanding."* [50] When freedom is reflective, our responsibility for self, others, and nature grows. Our freedom depends on the freedom of others. And the freedom of others depends on ours. In this way, we need to care for our relationships.

Stewart also points to Feuerbach, Hegel's student, who summarizes the master and slave dialectic when he notes that in our self-consciousness we are bound together; each of us reflects all human beings. Like the Tibetan monk Tich Nhat Han's famous 2004 poem, *Call Me By My True Names*, we come closer to seeing how we are inter-connected with all other humans as well as plants, insects, and all of nature. Our individual freedom is intricately related to the freedom of all people, members of all tribes, and all species.

The more aware we become of our interconnectedness, the more responsible we must be for our words and actions, and the freer. Atomic freedom lacks responsibility. For Stewart, it is opportunistic and reckless. In contrast, reflective freedom invites us *"to rethink the rights of labor and rights of property - and what to do when the two are in conflict. It calls for a new and better understanding of the actual sources of prosperity in human society."* [51]

Reflective freedom also aligns with Buber's I-Thou relationship in that it values seeing oneself in the other and the other in oneself for authentic and meaningful relationships. An ongoing tension exists between the values of atomic freedom (individual liberty, self-expression) and the values of reflective freedom (aspiration for conditions of fairness, equality, etc.) that allow all to be free to make moral choices.

Atomic and reflective freedoms can also be seen through the perspective of historian Tim Snyder who specializes in understanding authoritarian governments. In *On Freedom*, Snyder compares two ideas of freedom - negative and positive- that respectively mirror the atomic and reflective freedoms explained by Stewart. For Snyder, negative freedom is negative because it focuses on removing the obstacles to the individual liberty and mobility that "atoms" seek. It is concerned with the absence of oppression by removing barriers such as rules, regulations, and even government itself. Positive freedom, in contrast, is focused on creating conditions for flourishing. It shares the qualities of reflective freedom in that it asks us to consider what adds meaning to our lives. Positive freedom encourages us to create the conditions for flourishing so that we can be free to make moral choices. This is why Snyder calls positive freedom the "value of values."

Freedom is more than removing obstacles to do what we want regardless of how it affects others. Positive, reflective freedom makes it possible to realize other values. It involves co-creating a world through friendships across faith traditions where we treat all people and the planet with dignity and respect. If we are aware and careful, we can guide our tribes in choosing positive and reflective freedom as an end (while negative freedom is only a means to it). In this way, we belong to the World and flourish together.

Tip 3. Expand Your Mind

Rabbi Joseph H. Gelberman (z'l), my mentor for both the interfaith seminary and modern rabbi program, sensed an interspiritual religious landscape emerging when he quipped, *"Never instead of, Always in Addition to."* Rabbis Irwin Kula and Brad Hirschfeld echoed his motto when they acknowledged that an *either/or* mentality was no longer sufficient and that we needed to think in terms of *both/and*. We are inhabiting an age and a worldview that includes not only ourselves and our tribes but all tribes.

When we act in this world from a place of acceptance of others and in friendship with others from other tribes, our religions will, so to speak, appreciate, and our values will be more appreciated. The more we celebrate the fruitful teachings of all religions, the more we come to appreciate our own. The more we appreciate what all religions offer, the more we experience a world-centric worldview.

Both-And thinking helps us develop the capacity for intersubjective understanding that is needed to inhabit the mindset of the Interspiritual Age. Collective trauma therapist, Thomas Hubl, uses "playing in an orchestra" as a metaphor to explain intersubjectivity. As a member of an orchestra, one must be skilled at playing an instrument and be able to listen to others in the orchestra playing theirs. BOTH playing AND listening are needed *at the same time.* This expansion of presence allows for the harmonization of opposites, the next tip for belonging.

Tip 4. Harmonize Polarities

Extreme polarities divide our culture today. They are not new, but the widening gap between them is. One polarity that has plagued traditional communities is the dichotomy between religion and science, faith and reason. A most prominent example of this tension is found in the debate between evolution and creation as exemplified in the Scopes Trial of 100 years ago. When a high school teacher was accused of violating a Tennessee state law that banned teaching human evolution in public schools, the trial brought to the foreground the tension between a fundamentalist worldview (where the Bible took priority over scientific knowledge) and a modernist worldview (knowledge derived from science taking priority over the Bible). This debate plays out in politics to this day. While Congress debates over the separation of church and state, there are scholars finding harmony between the wisdom of spiritual mystics across religions and the discoveries of quantum physics.

As we grow into the integral worldview, the capacity to hold multiple worldviews - traditional, modern, etc. - we learn how science and religion complement each other, if we support interdisciplinary research in this area. For example, in "The Study of Mystical Experiences [MEs] and Latour's Ontological Turn," André van der Braak, Comparative Philosophy of Religion professor at Vrije Universiteit Amsterdam, writes, *"The psychedelic renaissance of the past decades has given a new impetus to moving the study of MEs from the armchair (studying the writings of the mystics) to the lab (empirical research)."* (Philosophical Psychology, May 2025, p. 4) The writings of the mystics, often sources of religious beliefs and descriptions of interspiritual experiences, can be better understood through the lens of quantum science. Van der Braak argues that *"concepts of actor-networks and modes of existence make room for a different participatory approach to MEs that interprets them as participatory events rather than as the inner experiences of an isolated subject."* (p. 5). In other words, the Cartesian subject-object distinction that influenced Western thinking for centuries is no longer adequate to explain certain experiences. The polarization of subjects and objects yields to the intersubjective field for which quantum science may apply better.

In the Interspiritual Age, the gap between science and religion, as well as other polarities, are opportunities for harmonizing our understanding of each to reach a new level of understanding with integrated values.

Tip 5. Float and Swim For Rabbi Wolpe, floating takes faith. Floating in water is especially enjoyable after learning to swim or propelling ourselves through water. Floating is relaxing. It takes faith to be still in the water, to trust the current. Faith, Wolpe reminds us, expresses our trust in what we believe. We trust the water will hold us. If water is a metaphor for religion, and floating takes faith, then what does it take to swim?

It is one thing to float through religion (to rely on faith), it is another to move the waters of religion, with intention, in a certain direction. By swimming, we reconceptualize religion's purpose and prepare for the changing currents of life and reinterpretation of the waters in which we float and swim. To better understand this environment to swim with religion, we can develop the following skills:

Balance - *Can we bring our tribe with us to belong to the World?*

Stretching - *Can we stretch our minds into the new worldview?*

Propulsion - *Can we evolve religion forward with human culture?*

Technique - *Can we improve how we practice and teach religion?*

If floating takes faith, swimming takes *spirit*. We can use our spirit to motivate us to swim in the Interspiritual Age.

PART TWO

BRING YOUR TRIBE

"You can't open minds that are closed."
- My 95-year-old mother with dementia

On October 7, 2023, the massacre of 1,200 people in Israel (800 Israelis) and capture of over 200 mostly Israeli civilians by Hamas ignited a war. After two years of fighting, Gaza was destroyed. Many Jews are horrified by Israel's response. 70,000 Palestinians (and probably more) are now dead. For decades, many Jews have been convinced that Israel's military policy can never achieve co-existence or peace. These policies *-the occupation itself-* began with the founding of the state. With this war, many Israelis and Diaspora Jews believe Israel is defending the freedom of religion, but we are not truly free if our religion and way of life/culture is protected at the expense of another's. Instead, we remain trapped in the annihilation dynamic of victim and oppressor, lord and bondsman.

Many of us, Jews and other activists, have been calling out the harm committed in the name of Judaism. We have been silenced by the legacy Jewish establishment for doing so until things got so bad that the harm could no longer be ignored and one can no longer look away. If Israel's extremist right-wing government controls the narrative, the policies themselves trigger Jewish trauma, making it harder for Jews to reimagine Judaism without an uber-militarized Jewish State. Yet, no time is riper and more urgent than now to bring our tribe to a new vision of Judaism.

Why does October 7th matter?

Six days after October 7th, 2023, I begged my senior Israeli cousin to consider a different response. While self-defense is justified, what many saw coming was collective punishment. My Israeli Jewish friends could only see red. With their sense of invincibility damaged, rage and shame overtook their neural pathways. War became synonymous with justice. Yet, we need to hear alternative stories from revenge, different scripts, in order to choose otherwise, not next time, this time.

No one experiencing personal tragedy wants to hear or be reminded of another's so while I suggested a different script to my senior cousin, I did not share a story that shocked the world twice – first with the horror of violence that left ten Amish children dead, and again when the Amish community, including parents of the girls killed, publicly decided to forgive the gunman (who also killed himself). These parents showed up at the gunman's funeral to comfort *his* parents.[52] We need stories like this to make us stop and think before taking revenge. Even President Biden, right after October 7th, warned Israelis of US mistakes in the wake of 9/11. Yet this cautionary tale did not matter to most Israelis. The invasion of Gaza began almost immediately. Calls for a ceasefire erupted in earnest.

At a meeting of Christians, Jews and Palestinians, convened by a pastor soon after the war broke out, participants planned protests calling for a ceasefire. Afterall, who can think of making peace until violence stops? At the same time, how can violence stop if combatants can't see a viable way forward.

Jonathan Kuttab, a Palestinian American Christian human rights lawyer, director of Friends of Sabeel North America (FOSNA), and founder of Non-Violence International, supports peace while recognizing *the reality of the one state*. (see "Modern Israel?") His book, *Beyond the Two State Solution*, offers ideas for peace in Israel Palestine. Since he would be in town, I invited him to speak to a small, diverse group of educators -Jews, Palestinian, Christians, Muslims, Afghans, and Lebanese. One attendee's mother is Israeli.

By learning about Kuttab's vision for peace in Israel Palestine, I hoped we could develop ideas for helping if not advocating for America's teachers to include peacemaking in their curricula through two components: practical solutions and psychological *soul*utions.

For practical solutions, what if American students read Kuttab's book and discussed it in the classroom? What if they learned about grassroots peace movements between Israelis and Palestinians such as *Standing Together, A Land for All,* and *One State?* What if the media reported regularly and in detail on peace groups like the Parents *Circle - Families Forum, Combatants for Peace, The Villages Group, Breaking the Silence,* etc.? What if students learned from the success stories of S. Africa and N. Ireland? Wouldn't this inspire ideas for peace over war? Could teachers expose students to lessons about practical solutions in history and now, including in Israel Palestine? Perhaps such lessons would inspire American students in our polarized country. However, practical solutions (defined borders, fair elections, ceasefire treaties, etc.) are insufficient. Freedom for a better life cannot be realized without healing unhealed collective trauma and building relationships between conflicting parties. We need *soul*utions.

By the end of the evening, after Jonathan Kuttab spoke, we traded books. He gave me his autobiography so I could learn more about his life as a Palestinian and his people's trauma and I gave him my copy of *Wounds into Wisdom: Healing Intergenerational Jewish Trauma* by Rabbi Tirzah Firestone. We wanted to understand each other's collective, historical experiences. When we exchanged books, a heart connection was made.

For psychological *soul*utions, we need to understand each other. In addition to firsthand accounts of Palestinians in the West Bank village of Umm al Khair (see "Reparations"), I read *In This Place*

Together: A Palestinian's Journey to Collective Liberation (Penina Eilberg-Schwartz, Suleiman Khatib), *The General's Son* (Peled), and *The 100 Years War on Palestine* (Khalidi), among other books and articles. I gained a deeper understanding of Palestinian trauma. In addition, I attended the online annual ceremony of bereaved parents in Israel Palestine who shared their stories and pain together. Not only was there ongoing cultural and historical trauma for Palestinians and Israelis living there but they and Diaspora Jews carried the historical trauma of the Holocaust and centuries of persecution. So, while I am haunted by Nazis, a Jewish Israeli friend is haunted by Hamas terrorists and Palestinians are haunted by Israeli settlers and soldiers. How can our collective traumas be healed?

In January 2024, six weeks after hosting Kuttab, my local public school district approved a resolution calling for a bilateral ceasefire in the Israel-Hamas war while also encouraging teachers to discuss the conflict in their classrooms. Here was an opportunity. Perhaps the school board would be interested in teaching practical solutions (like Kuttab's ideas and others') and psychological *soul*utions - approaches to healing the trauma on both sides. Rather than reinvent the wheel, was there an existing curriculum to which these ideas could be added?

I reached out to Tanenbaum, a nonprofit organization combating religious prejudice that offered programs to public school teachers, primarily Social Studies and Language Arts. *Transforming Conflict* seemed like a perfect fit. I met with the program directors. They were happy to share existing material with teachers in my group. Unfortunately, the material was not up to date for dealing with the current crisis which was understandable given the timing. Still, most teachers did not have a safe way to talk about the conflict in Israel Palestine. Even the word 'ceasefire' (let alone genocide) triggered fears of antisemitism in the Jewish community. This resulted in further internal obstacles to understanding. While ignorance could be a factor, the biggest block was denialism.

In *States of Denial,* sociologist Stanley Cohen identifies 3 types of denial: literal *(it never happened)*; interpretive *(it's not what you think it is, "it's complicated")*; and, implicative *(we must do it/it's terrible, but it's not our fault)*. The latter covertly suppresses the psychological, political and moral implications of what's being denied. Right after the war broke out, some of the work of Gabor Mate, the Hungarian-born, Canadian physician specializing in long term effects of trauma, went viral on social media. His Jewish background gave him credibility to name and explain the results of denialism. It was, he said, like "watching Auschwitz on TikTok."[53] He prescribed healing based on his personal and professional experience. Facing denial is part of *soul*utions, the inner work that we, as individuals, as members of a tribe, and as a society must go through, to heal ancient and raw scars. Yet even words dressed in metaphor and satire, literary tools to jar us awake (see "Can Barby Save Israel? PS And the US?"), fall short when denialism and revenge take over.

I called out *(tochecha)* to my fellow Jews through art, hoping to raise our awareness. I designed a digitally printed lithophane, "modern" charity *(tzedakah)* box with a light source to illuminate images on its four sides:
(1) a drawing of two children, one with a *kippah* (Jewish head covering) and one with a *keffiyeh* (Bedouin head scarf), in arms of friendship, (2) a 3-D topographical map of the land of Israel Palestine, (3) an Israeli flag and a Palestinian flag with the branches and roots of an olive tree superimposed over them, and (4) the text of a Jewish midrash and an Arabic poem about light and hope in English, Hebrew, and Arabic. Instead of dropping coins into a slot on the top of the *Peace in Israel Palestine (PIP) Luminary*, one scans QR codes for websites that link to Israeli and Palestinian grassroots peace movements (see image at this essay's end).

Calling out those who do harm is the first step of *Tochecha*. Hearing how I/we may have harmed others is the second. While I have been morally harmed by others in my community, I had to ask myself if I harm fellow Jews when my rebuke is *charged with anger?* Yes. It took time for me to realize that my anger is a cover for disappointment, sadness, and shame. Shame for failing to stop this war (as though I alone could do so), for failing to save the hostages (Israeli Jewish civilians held underground in Gaza *and* Palestinian civilians held in Israeli jails), and for failing to protect Palestinian friends in the West Bank killed in the name of Judaism. I am learning that my shame is based on a belief that I could have stopped the harm when in fact, I was helpless. The healing journey is both personal and collective. It involves repentance *(teshuvah)* and reparations *(tikkun)*. Together, with others, we are not helpless. In solidarity with others, we can stop violence and make amends. But we can't do it from the same worldview that created the problem. We need to step together into the integral worldview of the Interspiritual Age and accomplish the work.

Displaying the *PIP Luminary* as a ritual object in interfaith gatherings drew positive responses. In Jewish spaces, it tended to be ignored. As an educational tool, one Jewish group declined to use it for fear it was too political while a Palestinian shared that the war must stop before peace can even be an aspiration. While this piece and others were welcomed at a Jewish Exhibit Commemorating One Year After October 7, another year of war has passed. Of course, Jews are not the only "tribe" to suffer.

The Israel-Hamas War's impact on the Palestinian people has extended the pain of their original trauma (the *Nakba*) and will have devastating outcomes for generations to come. It will also be "a stain on Judaism," as declared by Rabbi Dr. Ismar Schorsch, the chancellor emeritus of The Jewish Theological Seminary (JTS) and the Rabbi Herman Abramovitz Distinguished Professor of Jewish history, in an interview with Peter Beinart on August 27, 2025. The ethno-centric and Messianic ideas of political Zionism led to a genocide. This claim is the conclusion of a growing number of genocide scholars, including Israeli Professor Omer Bartov, who titled his article in the *New York Times* on July 15, 2025, *I'm a Genocide Scholar. I Know It When I See It*. The religious nationalism of Zionism has run amok.

Howard Zinn (1922-2010), renowned American historian, called nationalism the greatest danger to humanity.[54] There is nothing wrong with pride in nation or tribe(s) but everything wrong with claiming superiority. "Do not be like other nations," the teachings of the Torah warn. Do not become empires that oppress others for you know what it is like to be oppressed. Such nationalism diminishes aspirations of Tim Snyder's positive freedom, freedom for something better for all. Indeed, it nourishes negative freedom, a desire to be free of obstacles in order to do as one pleases even if it harms others and lacks meaning.

How do we bring our tribes to a new worldview?

As I despaired over how to bring my tribe to a worldview that embraces the humanity of all people along with recognizing our interdependency, including with Palestinians, I remembered the words of a friend who said, *"Don't think of your tribe as holding you back or that you must leave your tribe behind. Think of what you're doing as holding up the rear."*

Holding up the rear is patience (see "Loving Ducks"). It means staying behind so no one is left out while *at the same time* experimenting with new forms and bringing the fruits of those experiments to the tribe so we all might evolve together. It means having faith, bearing witness, engaging in spiritual activism (see "Reparations: Spiritual Activism") as we transcend into a new worldview. Holding up the rear does not allow for denialism. It demands calling out the harm *(tochecha)* and repairing it.

To bring our tribes to the Interspiritual Age is to focus on our tribe - *not* reduced in historical, cultural, religious or ethnic terms but uplifted in human, universalist terms. In other words, I succeed when I see the members of my tribe not as Americans or Israelis or another nationality, not as Zionists or anti-Zionists, and not even as Jews, but as human beings who are hurt and trying to find safety. Traumatized and morally injured, we need agency to solve/resolve our political and psychological stalemates. Similarly, Palestinians are human beings who are hurt and trying to find safety. Traumatized and morally injured, they need agency to solve/resolve political and psychological stalemates. We can and must give each other agency, indeed, sovereignty. For a core Jewish value is that as human beings, we are made in the image of the Divine, and this wisdom should make us want to treat each other with dignity and respect and to confer the recognition of the other that leads to positive freedom for all. It should make us run towards doing so.

Interestingly, our tradition offers the spiritual tools to help us see ourselves and others as divinely created human beings deserving of recognition and agency. But words and actions are not enough. *We need new institutions that teach through new forms for "belonging to the World," for reframing our traditions through an integral lens.*

Two years after I approached them about a curriculum with "solutions and *soulu*tions," I was pleased to learn that Tanenbaum now offers a lesson called Peace in Practice, highlighting a narrative approach to teaching empathy (for both sides) in the Israeli Palestinian conflict. The lesson includes a video from the Parents Circle of bereaved mothers sharing their pain and healing their trauma by integrating their loss into resilient strength through solidarity. It comes from seeing the other and being seen. Teachers can now feel more supported by taking on this subject. This is an example of change in the way we teach that reflects the values of the Interspiritual Age, including holding more than one worldview at a time and finding our shared humanity in that space.

Another example of successful change is in the growing awareness of healing collective trauma. Two years after the war began, a few therapists in my Jewish community offered free workshops on intergenerational trauma. I imagine workshops being made available to all communities suffering from collective trauma. For Jews are not the only ones to suffer. *What if* healing unhealed trauma was a matter of public health? *What if* repairing moral harm through truth and reconciliation councils was a norm? *What if* unaddressed annihilation dynamics -*victim becomes perpetrator becomes victim*- are addressed as a priority?

Before reading the chapters in Part Two, clarity is needed around the term Zionism. The results of a survey by Political Science Professor Mira Sucharov of Carleton University in Ottawa, Canada are instructive. Sucharov conducted a study of American Jews' identification with Zionism. Without providing any definition of Zionism, 58% of respondents identified as Zionists, 10% as anti-Zionist and 12% as non-Zionist. She then used three different definitions. According to the first definition, *Zionism is the belief in a Jewish and democratic state,* 71% said they were Zionist. With the second definition, *Zionism means an emotional attachment to the state of Israel,* 71-72% also identified as Zionist. With the third definition, *Zionism is the privileging of Jews over non-Jews in Israel,* a definition expressing the experience of Palestinians; only 10% of American Jews surveyed identified as Zionist. Sucharov concluded that many American Jews who think they are Zionist may, in fact, not be, once they understand its ideology as oppression.

I have used the term "political Zionism" to describe the ideology behind Zionism (the third definition above) that results in the Palestinian experience of occupation, oppression and ethnic cleansing for Jews to have a Jewish-majority state with a procedural (not liberal) democracy. For this reason, according to this definition, I do not identify as a Zionist, nor do I equate Zionism with Judaism.

Finally, let me say that in February 2023, I led a Shabbat service for a local Jewish congregation. In my talk, I called out the harm of political Zionism to the collective soul of the Jewish people. I shined a light on the dark night of the Jewish soul whose internal dividedness felt like a fracture at the time. After October 7th, a complete break in Jewish unity may be imminent. In her sermon, *Everything is Breaking: Is Healing Even Possible?* delivered on November 1, 2025, Rabbi Sharon Brous of Ikar in Los Angeles, described the very real possibility of a "breakup," a complete schism of the collective Jewish community.

Unless... Unless we belong to the World and bring our tribes.

Part Two is a plea to my fellow Jews to grow with our ethno-centric (traditional) values, individual-centric (modern) values, and pluralistic (postmodern) values into a new worldview that contains the best of former values and allows new values to take root. It is a call to heal from the calcified layers of collective trauma. It is an honest request for reckoning and repair that can only take place if and as we evolve.

THE PIP LUMINARY
Peace in Israel Palestine
Shining Light on Grassroots Solutions

Scan the QR codes to learn how *civilian Israelis and Palestinians* are *jointly* transforming conflict into peace.

One Democratic State Campaign
One Equal State

A Land for All
Confederacy

Standing Together
Plural Consensus

NonViolence International
Beyond the Two State Solution

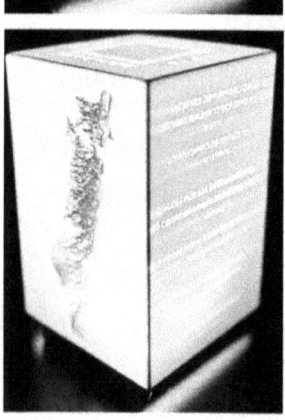

①
JUDAISM'S GIFT: EXILE AND RETURN

In *God Is Not One*, Stephen Prothero, Professor Emeritus of Religion in America at Boston University, explores the distinctive problems each major religion tries to solve and the unique solutions they offer. For Christianity, the problem is "sin" and the solution is "salvation." For Islam, "pride," and "submission." For Hinduism, the problem is "*samsara*" (birth, death, rebirth). The solution, *moksha* (liberation), is realizing the unity of self and the Divine. For Judaism, the problem is "exile," the solution is "return."

In Jewish history, exile *(Galut)* is everywhere. God sends Adam, Eve, Noah, Abraham, and Moses away. In addition, Assyrians, Babylonians, Romans, and more have forced the migration of the Israelites. The quintessential exilic drama, the story of Adam and Eve, is our Jewish legacy. The hope of Return to the Garden of Eden is our hope of Return to God. Redemption is our ticket out of exile. But exile and return (indeed, all the problems and solutions in Prothero's schema) present a paradox. Does being Jewish *depend* on being in exile? (Does being Hindu *depend* on samsara?)

For Jews, if exile ends, what then is our gift, our purpose, as Jews?

If Exile is a physical separation from a homeland, are those of us who go to live in this homeland still in exile? Politically, no. Zionism claimed to end Jewish exile. Theologically, no. Jews living in Israel achieved their return. Jews living in the Diaspora however remain in exile. Part of this exile is due to the relationship of diasporic Jews to Jews in Israel. Diasporic Judaism tends to be denigrated by Israeli Jews as less authentic. E.g., diasporic Jews must celebrate two Seders on Passover to make up for this lessness while Israeli Jews celebrate only one. Today, as most Jews around the world are now living in Israel, says Josh Leifer in *Tablets Shattered*, Israeli Jews feel even more entitled to dismiss American Jewish practice. In fact, according to Leifer, as some American

Jews call for the decoupling of Judaism from Zionism, so too do many Israeli Jews call for the severance of ties with the Judaism of America if not with American Jews. Polarization is appearing in all corners of world. With today's political Zionism, the value of Judaism's exile, as Prothero imagines it, is lost.

Return (*teshuvah*), for me, is about closeness with God and the experience that comes with making all of life holy, with raising the sparks of Divinity that were shattered when God created the world, according to the parable of Rabbi Isaac Luria (1534-1572). Judaism, I thought, valued repairing the world *(tikkun olam)*, justice and charity *(tzedakah)*, and loving-kindness *(chesed)* through praying, chanting, studying and the practice of the commandments *(mitzvot)* for making the world a better place *for all*. If return is not possible, then Judaism needs to redefine its mission. If it is possible, then Judaism needs exile to achieve return.

How can other religious practitioners learn from Judaism (as well as other traditions) about return *(teshuvah)* if Jews no longer live in or experience exile? We experience return *because* we experience exile, a separation from God, Oneness, Nonduality. We are exiled from experiencing oneness with God, not from experiencing separation from a particular piece of land, *ha-aretz (the land)*.

In *The Necessity of Exile,* Shaul Magid argues for preserving exile in Jewish life. Diminishing or erasing it comes at a cost to our identity. Political Zionism then undermines Judaism's special gift. Thus, Magid argues for a "counter-Zionism" that allows us to be in exile in the diaspora *and* in Israel. Reclaiming exile (and thus return) can help us uncouple Zionism from Judaism.[55] This gives us a chance to archive our Israel-centric Judaism, or Israelism,[56] and our ethno-centric form of religion, with the history of Judaism. In turn, we make room for a new Judaism *detached from political Zionism*, a Judaism that can flourish in the Interspiritual Age.

What is Judaism if it is detached from Zionism?

For many Jews around the world, Zionism and Judaism are the same. This is problematic for the task of bringing our tribe to belong to the World. In *Tablets Shattered*, Joshua Leifer writes, *"Israel is the assimilation of Judaism into the oppressive nation-state form that caused so much of Jewish suffering such that Judaism has become homeless itself."* (p. 215) Judaism itself is in exile. The parable of *The Rooster Prince* by Rabbi Nachman of Breslov (1772-1810), founder of the Breslov form of Hasidism, might help us.

The Rooster Prince
A young prince thinks he is a rooster, takes off his clothes, sits naked under the table, and pecks at his food on the floor. Horrified by his behavior, the king and queen call in experts to convince the prince to act human again. Nothing works. Then a new wise person comes to the palace. He takes off his clothes and sits naked under the table with the prince, claiming to be a rooster, too. Gradually the prince accepts him as a friend. The wise man tells the prince that a rooster can wear clothes, and so the prince puts on clothes. After a while, the wise man tells the prince he can eat at the table, and eventually that he can act human. Gradually, the Rooster Prince accepts each idea and step-by-step, begins to be human again, until he is fully cured.

Have today's Zionists become the Rooster Princes of our age?

Today, Jews are exiled not by "God" (like Adam and Eve) or by "others" (a history of persecutors) but by us. As Wendy Elisheva Somerson explains in *An Anti-Zionist Path to Embodied Jewish Healing*, anti-Zionist Jews who see Zionists oppressing Palestinians may choose not to identify with their tribe at all, or to distance themselves from Jews and Jewishness altogether. The danger of this response, what Leifer calls renunciation, is that it cedes Jewishness to Zionism forestalling our return to Judaism albeit in a new form. But return can be achieved by facing the trauma we carry and healing as a path to our return. It entails getting under the table with our *rooster princes*, the ethno-centric parts of ourselves that we imagine can save us. In today's reality, the weaponization of antisemitism and the equivalency of Judaism with Zionism makes Jews more vulnerable. Healing our rooster identities means sitting with those parts of ourselves that no longer serve us. It means healing, individually, with our tribes, and in interspiritual groups where we recognize the trauma of others.

What would it look like if Jewish institutions recognized the public health threat of not healing the intergenerational trauma that feeds the annihilation dynamic? What if Jewish Federations funded trauma healing programs instead of Birthright trips? Would we not be practicing the Jewish gift of spiritual exile and return?

On August 17, 2025, during the virtual vigil, *We Will Not Look Away,* a program on grief in the face of genocide attended by hundreds of people around the world, co-presenter Rabbi Lynn Gottlieb invoked Jewish attendees to remember that Judaism existed long before Zionism. Our job is to stop Zionism, she said, and return to Judaism. She also said that it is only through solidarity with others that we collectively heal and become liberated. The other, in this case, includes Palestinians.

The question remains as to what kind of Judaism we will return. We need new forms for teaching and practicing Judaism, new Jewish spaces, new Jewish institutions. These forms can be relevant to Jews around the world, both in the diaspora *and* in Israel, as Magid claims, but we need to create them with the consciousness of a new worldview and thereby literally create a new world. I call it Interspiritual.

② JEWISH IDENTITY, AGAIN

The conclusions of the Pew Research Center's Religion & Public Life Project of 2013,[57] the first major survey of *American Jews* in over a decade at that time, confounded me and my students, who were children of Jewish intermarriage. The data showed that intermarriage continued to rise and that fewer Jews raised children with a Jewish identity. Of the "Jews of no religion" who had children at home, two-thirds did not raise their children Jewish in any way. This contrasted with "Jews with religion" of whom 93 percent said they were raising children with a Jewish identity. Jewish leaders responded by ringing the alarm bells.

An American Jewish history professor at Jewish Theological Seminary said the results showed *"a very grim portrait of the health of the American Jewish population in terms of their Jewish identification."* Then-Editor in Chief of *The Jewish Daily Forward,* found the results *"devastating"* and thought American Jews would have cared more about religion. *"This should serve as a wake-up call for all of us as Jews,"* she warned. Then-Deputy Director of the Pew Religion Project said, *"It's very stark"* and commented, *"Older Jews are Jews by religion. Younger Jews are Jews of no religion."* The report concluded by saying that *"...this secular trend had serious consequences for what Jewish leaders called Jewish continuity."*

Which leaders? What did they mean "not Jewish in any way"? Was Jewish *identity and continuity* threatened or just their *idea* of it? What if something else was going on?

It has been 13 years since that report came out and Jews did not disappear. As is evident from the more recent Pew Study of 2024, Judaism is not threatened with extinction by rising intermarriage rates or religious disaffiliation. In fact, in the decade since Pew's 2014 Religious Landscape Study, little has changed in the rate of "mixed religious marriages" that have stayed steady at a quarter of married adults. The rise of religious nones has also leveled off.[58]

Perhaps our leaders got it wrong. Perhaps interfaith marriages kindled a new way of *becoming Jewish* that is *not yet evident*.

Both the 2014 and 2024 Pew Studies ask questions from the reality frame of an ethno-centric worldview. Thus, they miss the evolution occurring beneath the surface. As Susan Katz Miller notes in her blog about the 2024 survey,

> *"The question that Pew continues to ask in these surveys, 'What is your present religion, if any?' uses the singular 'is' and immediately sets a tone discouraging anyone from checking more than one box. The dominant exclusivist mindset –the research framework– that says everyone must have one, and only one, religious identity continues to deform and erase those who claim multiple religions."* [59]

The 2013 snapshot of American Jewish identity also showed changes in how Jews think of other religions. *"In a surprising finding, 34 percent said you could still be Jewish if you believe that Jesus was the Messiah."* For interfaith families, this is not surprising. Marriage to people of different traditions is full of inter-religious paradoxes and contradictions that result in new understanding about other religions and one's own. Susan Katz Miller's study of adult children raised with and educated in two religions sheds light on the promise of interfaith education, one of which is the extent to which these children grow up to be peacemakers and conflict resolvers as discussed earlier.[60]

Interfaith relationships provide opportunities to work through theologically contradictory beliefs. The result is not *"young people with no religion"* but young people with… something else. It may not look familiar, it may not be the same as our ancestors' practice, but that doesn't mean something Jewish isn't happening. Regular inter-religious conversations, interfaith social justice projects, multifaith prayer opportunities - these may be the outlines of a burgeoning Jewish identity in the Interspiritual Age, one that makes praying with people of other traditions feel normal. The survey also found that despite declines in formal religious identity and participation, American Jews were proud to be Jewish with a strong sense of belonging to the Jewish people.

We are moving to a banner for Judaism that values *Integrity and Connection* over the old banner of *Identity and Continuity*. What we measure in future surveys will help determine if we see it. Thus, instead of asking, "Did you visit a Jewish Museum this past year?" a survey that reflects the worldview of the Interspiritual Age might ask the following:

"Did you visit a Jewish Museum *with someone of another faith* this year?"

"Did you visit a cultural museum with someone who identifies with that culture this past year?"

"Did you share something about Judaism with a person of another faith this past year?"

"Did you learn something from someone of another faith this past year?"

"Did you visit a multifaith worship center this past year?"

"Did you engage in an activity of solidarity with Jews and non-Jews this past year?"

As the joke goes, I've got good news and bad. The good news is Judaism survives. The bad news is you won't recognize it. Where Jews go, Judaism follows. We, the people, are the evolutionary agents that make religions change, as we always have.

Where Jews are going is not a return to the past, not to a form of Judaism *before* Zionism but to something new. In *Tablets Shattered*, Josh Leifer quotes Rabbi Alissa Wise, a former leader of Jewish Voice for Peace, who observed *"Jewish particularism is on the wane, but Jewish practice as a way to connect wider and wider is on the rise."* Leifer criticizes this "practice without particularism" for its lack of *"what progressives' recoil from: the tradition's difficult obligations; the priority of familial and ethnic ties."* (p. 265) This criticism represents the traditional worldview. The Interspiritual Age is one where wider interconnected community of all religions respect and support each other in practicing their traditions and celebrating the familial and ethnic ties Leifer personally settles on. But now Jews won't be independent of others; they will be *inter*dependent. In this way, we bring and evolve with our tribes. Let me offer an example of interdependent identity formation from the *Shomeret Shalom* chapbook by Rabbi Lynn Gottlieb.

The following is an example of *interdependency* between Jewish and Indigenous with respect to each tradition's cultural and ethnic ties. Gottlieb explains, *"As we [Jews] explore how to put Indigenous Land Back teshuvah into practice, we must create new halachot (protocols) to guide our relationship to indigenous cultural, economic and spiritual production... to determine what is and is not kosher, that is, fit for use in relation to Indigenous peoples' way of life."* (p. 71)

When it was trending for non-indigenous people to use white sage (a sacred plant in Indigenous culture) for ritual purposes, it was decided that it was not to be used or poached off the land. But it was also decided that it was permissible for non-indigenous people *"to benefit from the aroma and the blessing of restored land... even if you grow white sage in your backyard, smudging is sacred to indigenous people and gerim (colonial settlers) should not use it in ritual without expressed permission from local Indigenous stewards of the land."* (p. 71) In this way, reparations are being made to Indigenous people and their land. Respect for other traditions becomes part of repair *(tikkun olam)*, a Jewish social justice practice. Gotlieb continues, *"It is a blessing to be smudged in ceremony by Indigenous prayer leaders and to receive a gift of sacred plants."* (p. 71) Such blessings are bestowed when we show respect for another's culture. In turn, Indigenous people receive the blessings of the Jewish tradition of return and repair *(teshuvah and tikkun)*.

We can all participate in a wider interconnection between religions that both preserves the traditions of each while sharing our wisdom and blessings. Doing so expands our worldview. When religious tribes show respect for each other's traditions in a multi-cultural world, we develop our *interdependent* identity. This is Interspiritual.

③

ROADMAP TO NO OTHER LAND

When *No Other Land (2024)* won Best Documentary Film in 2025, I was reminded of a similar film, *Roadmap to Apartheid (2012)*. In both films, one hears the cry, *Justice for All,* from both Israelis and Palestinians. But only if we listen - and we cannot listen if the films are boycotted as both were by distributors unwilling or too afraid to show them. Palestinian Israeli Sami Abu Shehadeh explained that *Justice For All* is exactly what Palestinians want.[61] But in March 2023, Israeli protesters marching against Netanyahu's judicial reforms squandered an opportunity to march with Palestinians for *justice for all*. Did both films fail to move the cultural evolutionary needle?

Roadmap to Apartheid compared Israel with South Africa during its apartheid regime. The film was made by a Jewish Israeli and a white South African. Similarly, *No Other Land* was made by a Palestinian and an Israeli. It tells a similar story, twelve years later with different details. Unlike *Roadmap to Apartheid, No Other Land* won an Oscar. In their acceptance speech at the Academy Awards ceremony, the filmmakers announced, *"We made this film, Palestinians and Israelis, because our voices are stronger together. We see each other."*[62] Yet, the opportunity for others, including Jews, to literally see the film was limited to independent theaters.

When *Roadmap* premiered in 2013, only a few Jews attended. Given the Pew survey of the time, in which 43% of Jews said *"caring about Israel"* is *"an essential part of what being Jewish means to them"* and 69% *"felt an emotional attachment to Israel,"* most Jews who knew about it chose to boycott the film.[63] In contrast, when I saw *No Other Land*, a Jewish member of the audience approached me afterwards to say he would not have known about the film were it not for the Academy Awards. He was shocked by what he saw and embarrassed, even ashamed. But not all Jews saw it.

Both films threaten Jews who hold a dominant ethno-centric worldview. When our models for Jewish education loyally support that worldview, it becomes difficult to grow into our expanding consciousness. For this reason, as part of an interspiritual approach to teaching Judaism, I brought students and parents to the premiere of *Roadmap to Apartheid* in 2013 and encouraged people in my Jewish circle to see *No Other Land* in 2025.

What prevents Jews from an openness to seeing these films?

When ethnonationalist religious identity is based on oppression of others through military power, a wall covers the heart and arrests compassion for the oppressed. In fact, studies show an inverse relationship between power and empathy. (The more power, the less empathy.) So, it's important to understand how the historical trauma of genocide against the Jewish people is trapped in the Jewish psyche. When trauma is not properly healed, it comes out in ways that harm self and others. A healing of the entire Jewish community is called for to prevent Jews from committing against others the very crimes our ancestors endured. This healing can't happen until the current crimes stop. As Jews, we can benefit from recognizing this and doing the therapeutic work of releasing the grip in which unhealed trauma locks us. In addition, we can practice Judaism from a world-centric perspective that lets our Jewish identity align with human integrity over tribal loyalty. What might *Integrity Over Identity* look like when teaching Judaism in The Interspiritual Classroom? Here is one snapshot.

When my students analyzed different indicators of Jewish identity in a survey of New York's Jewish population, they found that one indicator was "standing up to antisemitism." Tobias (age 14) responded, "Standing up to antisemitism doesn't mean you're Jewish, it means you're a good person." The lesson is: Everyone can and should stand up to injustice whenever they see it, not because of being Jewish but because it is the right thing to do as a human being with *integrity*. Jews need others to combat antisemitism as much as others need Jews to stand up for them. Today, as Jews, we should be rushing to films like *Roadmap to*

Apartheid and *No Other Land* and standing up against anti-Palestinianism[64], even, and especially, if it comes from our own tribe.

When Jesse Jackson told a crowd of Muslim Americans shortly after 9/11 that they could fight for Muslim civil rights or they could fight for *everyone's* civil rights, they got the message. He made it clear, said Eboo Patel, founder of Interfaith America, that all the marches and freedom rides of the civil rights movement were not to keep blacks from being sent to the back of the bus but to prevent *anyone* from being sent to the back of the bus.[65] This is an example of a faith-based community leading the way with world-centric integrity. For Zionists, the cry of *Never Again* after the Holocaust became *Never Again for Jews*. But for Jews adopting a world-centric morality, we can and must ensure that no people suffer genocide. We must declare *"Never Again means Never Again for Everyone."*

Ethno-centric identity can inform integrity, but when it comes to the interspiritual classroom, integrity has more weight. Why? Because if we want to say "No" to something wrong and that wrongdoing stems from us, then we're stuck. Stepping outside of identity through integrity releases us to act.

After *Roadmap to Apartheid*, my students and I stayed for a "Q & A". Barbara Harvey, a Jewish American lawyer and human rights advocate, and Sam Bahour[66], a Palestinian and American businessman, responded to audience questions with facts and personal reflections. Sam summarized all that he and his father's generation had done to get international attention on injustices suffered by Palestinians under Israeli control – from recognizing the State of Israel to recognizing the State of Palestine. Nothing worked. Then he shared what his teenage daughter at that time and her generation suggested, namely, tell Israel, *"You win. Let Israel have all the land, air, and coast, so long as WE come with it."*

The implications of this shift in perspective were enormous. When Palestinians and Israelis leap from *their* rights to *everyone's* rights, a groundswell of support for *Equal Rights for All Who Inhabit the Land* (no matter what religion or status) can emerge en masse.

Ethno-centric minded Israelis and Palestinians may feel they lost their tribe's nationalistic dreams. But each will gain something better together - freedom from mutual bondage and this can lead to peace, equality, justice and joy. To quote from *Roadmap to Apartheid*, *"It is possible!"*

The possibility of liberation for Israelis and Palestinians comes out of a movement of solidarity. This nonviolent struggle is driven by a growing intersection of communities around the world. Not only ethnic, religious, and native Indigenous tribes, but also queers, feminists, workers, BIPOC, artists, celebrities, and more. Equality for all and the values of democracy are defining the next iteration of Judaism and hopefully all our world's religions. It reflects the social solidarity of the Interspiritual Age.

(4)
MODERN ISRAEL?

Does American Jewish identity revolve around Israel to the extent that every Jewish congregation, *minyan, havurah,* and *kehillah* in the United States will dissolve should Israel's "democracy" fall?

Daniel Gordis, an American-born Israeli author, hopes so. He said, *"The idea that a flourishing Jewish community can proceed without Israel as a core part of its identity is simply not realistic."* He also said, *"To tell you the truth, if Israel were destroyed, I hope it would be the end of the Jewish people."* [67] Gordis believes the *"mesmerizing and almost magical"* view of Israel held by many Americans despite the current war precludes a thriving Jewish diaspora. Besides failing to acknowledge the dark, idolatrous side of this hypnosis, Gordis lacks awareness of what's happening on the margins of American Jewish life. So I'd like to offer a different perspective because, as Tom Friedman wrote in his NYT Opinion piece, *"American Jews have to choose sides on Israel."*[68]

I suggest that this choice includes embracing a new Judaism, not a new religion, but a new form for Judaism. The seeds for a new Judaism are planted on American turf. They will grow, whether Israel fades or not. This new Judaism will animate American Jewish life and may even help Israel.

The mantra that Israel-the-state is a liberal democracy, long championed by American and Israeli Jews, is a myth. According to Israeli sociologist Sammy Smooha, "Israel is a *procedural* democracy, *not* a *liberal* democracy."[69] There is no constitution supporting a full bill of rights with equality for *all* of Israel's inhabitants. Israel's Entry Law prevents Arabs with Israeli citizenship from continuing to live in Israel with their spouse if they marry a Palestinian from the Occupied Territories. This is just one example. In short, the democracy Israelis support – for Jews only- is *not* a *liberal* democracy.

As Razi Nabluse noted, the protests in Israel in March of 2023 (before October 7th) was,

> the first time...there had been such a fundamental struggle over the structure and identity of [Israel] the state, specifically over limits of 'Jewish democracy,' as well as over the relationship of the state to Judaism as a religion, issues of personal freedom, and the kind of state that Jews want.[70]

If Israeli Jews fight for a true liberal democracy, they will have to face the occupation of Palestinians. Instead, in 2023, they said Palestinians were irrelevant to their rejection of Netanyahu's judicial overhaul. Strategically, they needed demonstrators and the least common denominator for the greatest turnout meant supporting a Jewish-Only democracy. Yet, Israel's Supreme Court is not known for protecting human rights.[71] Continuing as an illiberal democracy meant Palestinians would keep suffering from human rights abuses at the hands of Israeli soldiers, settlers, police, and judges, forcing many Diaspora Jews to reassess what exactly mesmerizes them about Israel.

Rania Hammad and Jonathan Ofir pointed out the anti-government protest movement's aim was to preserve the status quo when they wrote,

> An apartheid state cannot be a democracy, and no number of blue and white flags can erase that fact. The oppression of the Palestinians will always be at the center of this problem, and ignoring it merely means prolonging the pain and the dehumanization. How Israel treats and relates to Palestinians is and will define what it is and what it becomes. Therein lie both its predicament and its redemption. [72]

Until this relationship is rectified, until Palestinian rights are *also* recognized, the magic of Israel will evaporate for Jews in and out of Israel. Jewish tradition obligates Jews to help the stranger, and this includes Palestinians, Bedouin and all non-Jewish inhabitants of the land. Jews can no longer dodge the incongruency of the state of Israel and the religion of Israel.

In the spring of 2023, Israelis and Palestinians could have become allies; they could have allied to co-create a true liberal democracy with a constitution, bill of rights, and government protecting freedom of religions and cultures for all throughout the land. As a liberal democracy, Israel could increase opportunities for intercultural and interfaith contact to lead the larger community from conflict to cooperation, and from brokenness to wholeness. They missed this opportunity and I wonder if it will go down as a moment of folly in Jewish history.

Rather than recognize the potential for empowering Palestinians in the crisis, Gordis (and other Israeli leaders) tapped into the Jewish fear that without Israel, there is no safe haven for Jews or Judaism. This fear keeps Jews from criticizing Israeli policies even when those policies upend Jewish values. Gordis triggers this fear when he quotes Charles Krauthammer,[73] *"'Israel is the hinge. Upon it rest the hopes—the only hope—for Jewish continuity and survival.' Everywhere."*

For many American Jews, the failure to raise their ranks among the next generation (excluding Orthodox Jews with higher birth rates) compared to the number of Jews now living in Israel means that the Judaism of Israel, if it is *the hinge*, has failed the diaspora, not the other way around. Whether Israel remains an illiberal democracy, evolves into a liberal one or continues to devolve into a theocratic, ethno-fascist state, Judaism itself needs a new center, a new frame of reference.

To survive, Judaism must change. Many Jews desire to experience Judaism differently. Indeed, the number of anti-Zionist Jewish congregations in America is growing. Survival is less about *continuity* and more about *connection*. It is less about Jewish identity requirements dictated by a chief rabbi and more about developing integrity as human beings. I was pleased when I learned about the *Interfaith Movement for Human Integrity,* an organization chaired and founded by Rabbi Lynn Gottlieb. The following quote by a Palestinian in the West Bank as recorded by Rabbi David Cooper makes the point. *"Ultimately there was no difference whether we were Jew or Arab, Israeli or Palestinian; what mattered was whether we acted with integrity."*[74] Perhaps, it is not the Jewish future that hinges on the fate of Israel but Israel's future that hinges on the fate of human evolution.

If diasporic Jews let Gordis' "modern Israel" define Judaism, the personal and collective soul of the Jewish people will divide. And, a divided soul, said Socrates, is the worst of all agonies. As one 26-year-old Jewish-identifying, anti-Zionist, American doctoral student told me, *"If Israel falls, at least American Judaism will be less morally compromised."* That trade-off comes from the fact that Zionism is less of a Jewish national liberation movement and more of a system of oppression for maintaining a strictly defined religious majority. Decoupling Judaism from Zionism could spur the development of a new form of Judaism – and relieve some of the Jewish agony.

A new form of Judaism (or of any religion) must meet the definition of evolution. It must *include what came before and transcend it (through integration) into a new form.* Judaism must reflect a *paradigm shift* in the way it reveals itself. It must show that a new level of consciousness, a new worldview, with new (and former) values is adopted by a large enough number of people to cross the tipping point into effectiveness and power. It must fill a need so great that it changes the way Jews relate to Judaism. Rabbinic Judaism as practiced since the destruction of the Second Temple is, today, no longer sufficient as a model for Jewish life. Rabbi Michael Strassfeld hit the nail on the head when he wrote, *"Rabbinic Judaism was meant to be portable; it could be carried wherever Jews traveled in the world. Now, we need a Judaism that is permeable allowing the outside world to easily interact with the inner world of Jewish life."*[75]

The seeds for this new Jewish way of life were planted in the soil of America's liberal democracy. These seeds will grow as Judaism detaches from political Zionism and transcends ethno-centrism. It will develop a world-centric form of liberal democracy and interspiritual solidarity.[76]

For decades, this new Judaism has been forming buds on the edge, where new growth usually begins. Perhaps it germinated when disillusioned American Jews began seeking spirituality in Eastern traditions (Rami Shapiro, Sylvia Boorstein, Bernie Glassman, etc.), or when intermarried American Jews experimented with "being both" (Miller) or taught Judaism with an interfaith orientation (Zinn) or when members of the Half-Jewish Network gave voice to a Universal Judaism (Margolis) or when an outcast orthodox rabbi founded interfaith seminaries (Gelberman).

Many of these Jewish pioneers were rejected by mainstream American Jewish institutions. From the sidelines, they carried on. Today, their efforts resonate with Jews searching for deep knowing, perennial wisdom, and the shared mystic heart found in all religions. They planted the seeds for a new vision of Judaism.

Spiritual Paths Institute founder, Ed Bastian, said, *"Religions come into contact to stimulate each [other] to regenerate their essential life force."* In other words, spiritual diversity, not insulated immersion, guarantees the evolution of our world's religions. Gordis may be right that Jewish life outside of Israel will die if Israel falls, but a healthier Judaism and Jewish society may be born. This new vision –nondual, interspiritual, universal, integral, inclusive, detached from political Zionism, aligned with liberal democracy, and open to learning alongside and from other religions– is coming into view. It may be *the last hope –the only hope–* not only for the diaspora but for Israel, too. *Israelis* will have to choose.

The choice before all Jews is whether we create the spaces and institutions for this new Judaism. If we do, I believe our grandchildren will thank us. And, as members of all our world's religious tribes choose to belong to the World of the Interspiritual Age, their descendants will also be grateful. In social solidarity we shall stand.

(5)
REPARATIONS: SPIRITUAL ACTIVISM

If you are a Jewish baby boomer, we probably have a lot in common: fond memories of family Seders, shabbat dinners, Jewish summer camps, trips to Israel, life on a kibbutz, or studying at Hebrew University. Some of us may have dated or married an Israeli, considered making *aliyah* (emigrating to Israel), taught Hebrew School, or celebrated an adult Bar, Bat, or B-Mitzvah. We may also share not-so-fond memories of feeling shunned by our community. Yet, we're still here. We stayed as members of our tribe even though, at times, we may have felt like outcasts. Why?

Perhaps we remain because, as Rabbi Adin Steinsaltz said, the Jewish people are, above all else, a family. Whether the members of our family are in Israel or the Diaspora, dead or alive, we care.

Yet, when our Jewish community marginalizes or shuns any of its members, it hurts us all. So, it's imperative we pay attention when people in our tribe feel unheard. One thing I've learned over the years is that *many of us*, at one time or another, have felt left out or rejected by our bigger Jewish family. Whether it was because we were divorced, widowed, 'still' single, intermarried, female, gay, trans, non-binary, disabled, a convert, Mizrahi, Ladino, BIPOC, multi-faith, too old, too young, too rich, too poor, we just wanted to feel validated by our tribe.

Decades ago, a particular form of shunning became apparent to me. In the early 2000's, I hosted a group of Jewish women at my house to hear Israeli Army Captain Rachel Persico (z'l) speak about injustices by Israelis towards Palestinians. She had firsthand experience. After facing years of discrimination and harassment for her intermarriage, Rachel, an Israeli and her Palestinian husband, left their homeland. The Jewish women in attendance became defensive and resisted the notion that Israel was racist. A non-Jewish social worker in the group explained how abuse can repeat and spread on a national scale. But because in Rachel's story *Jews* were the perpetrators, the Jewish women pushed back, leaving me and Rachel, who were concerned about Palestinian welfare and Israeli discrimination against Palestinians, pushed to the margins or even pushed out of the family altogether.

I think I also speak for others when I say I have felt silenced for decades by members of our community for questioning Israel's treatment of Palestinians and for educating others about it. I could list many examples, but instead I want to lift those Jews who experience the agony of a divided tribal soul, an agony intensified by the contradiction between Torah's teachings and the actions of many Israelis and Zionists in the name of Judaism. Borrowing from Rabbi Burt Jacobson, an apt name for those of us who recognize *our role in harming* and *our responsibility in helping* Palestinians, *and who do something about it,* is Spiritual Activist. Rabbi Burt Jacobson, who started Kehilla Community Synagogue in 1984 in Oakland, California, explains *spiritual activism* by quoting the Baal Shem Tov (1698-1760), mystic, healer and founder of Hasidic Judaism,

> *The real significance of the biblical teaching, 'And you shall love your neighbor as yourself,' hinges on the true meaning of the Hebrew word, 'k'mo'khah.' Usually k'mo'khah has been translated 'as yourself, but the Ba'al Shem renders it 'exactly like yourself.' In other words, even though we have distinct bodies, minds, and personalities, all human beings share a single spiritual essence. This obligates us to care for one another in a proactive way because we are all one.* [77]

We need spiritual activism to complement political activism. Both are necessary, said Rabbi Burt. Spiritual activism means being sensitive to the suffering of the persecuted *and* the persecutors. Spiritual activists recognize the dignity in each human being, and every human's right to feel a sense of belonging and home, *including* Palestinians. Spiritual activists aim to end all forms of violence *and* begin all ways of healing so that all may experience the dignity of being human. We all deserve to be treated with dignity and to treat others with dignity.

Reparations is a tool in the spiritual activist's toolbox.

In 2021, as part of his spiritual activism, Rabbi Burt Jacobson laid the groundwork with his congregation for starting *Face to Face: Jewish and Palestinian Reparations Alliance,* aka F2F. He said that *"Being a Spiritual Activist is a way for American Jews to ally with and support Palestinians in a face-to-face interpersonal way."* [78]

This face-to-face approach reminded me of my experience with a Palestinian in Jerusalem in 1980. Back then the term used was Arab. Each time I went to the Hebrew University pool, the same Arab locker attendant greeted me. Ibrahim was quiet, curious, and kind. We got to know each other during towel exchanges. When I mentioned I was looking for an onyx chess set for my father, he offered to take me to the Arab Market to find one. My Israeli Sephardic Jewish roommate warned me not to go. *"You cannot trust Arabs [Palestinians],"* she said. I trusted Ibrahim.

Our journey into the crowded *Shuk* (Arab market) was one of my most memorable experiences of that year. Ibrahim's family's hospitality stood out. I often wish we'd kept in touch. Perhaps I felt guilty that his family did not enjoy the same rights in Israel as mine. So, in late 2021, when I learned I could join a Jewish Palestinian Reparations group that would meet virtually with Palestinians in the West Bank, the tug on my heart was a resounding *yes*.

Rabbi Burt described *Jewish Reparations Allyship* as follows:

- taking on the struggle of Palestinians and Israeli activists as our own
- standing up for the Palestinians, even when we feel scared
- using the benefits of our privilege as American Jews to aid Palestinians
- acknowledging that while we, too, feel pain, the conversation is not about us; nonetheless, our work on behalf of the Palestinians can be healing for us as well
- being guided by the Palestinian villagers who will be engaged on the ground in the actual work of implementing the alliance, and by our Jewish activist partners in Israel

Do Jewish Reparations make a difference?

I'll share two stories and let you decide.

Story 1

Face to Face members met regularly via Zoom with our Palestinian contact in the Hebron Hills (Masafer Yata) of the West Bank. His name was Awdah Hathaleen. Awdah was a Bedouin schoolteacher, a young father of three small children by 2025. His village is only two meters from the closest settlement, separated by a barbed wire fence. On the settlers' side, there is green grass, unlimited water, pools, electricity for the community and chickens, schools, and freedom to move from settlement to settlement. On the Palestinian villagers' side, there is no running water, no electricity, no green grass, no pools, and no freedom of movement. Israeli soldiers demolish the villagers' cars and homes, regularly and repeatedly. Yet, the Palestinians remain steadfast in their desire and commitment to stay on their land. This is called *Sumud*.

In Spring of 2023, Awdah told us a hopeful story. One day, a group of young boys from the settlement (around age 13) stood by the fence watching Palestinian youth play soccer. Awdah asked the settler boys if they wanted to play. They said yes. Awdah told his community, *"We will not play Israelis against Palestinians, and we will not keep score. We will mix up the teams and play for fun."* But first, they had to figure out how to get the boys inside the village. They dug a hole under the fence so the Jewish settler boys could pass through. Then, they played soccer and it gave everyone hope. Later, the boys' parents found out and forbade them to ever come near the fence again.

When I asked my adult daughter what this story recalled, she immediately said, *"The Boy in the Striped Pajamas."* It's important to diverge for a moment to understand the reference. *The Boy in the Striped Pajamas* is a book and a movie (2008) of a story that takes place during WWII. A German boy named Bruno is alone during the day when his parents are busy. As he walks in the woods near his new home, he discovers a concentration camp. He does not know what it is or that his father oversees its gas chambers.

Through the barbed wire fence, Bruno befriends Shmuel, a Jewish boy too young to understand what's going on. Bruno thinks the people in the camp, even though they look hungry, are having fun because they wear striped pajamas all day. Lonely, he longs to join them. Eventually, Bruno *digs a hole under the fence to pass through to the other side*. Shmuel shows him the barracks where he can get striped pajamas. Suddenly, they are rounded up with others. As they enter a dark room, Bruno thinks it's all part of a big adventure, a surprise. His mother, searching for her missing son, realizes where he's gone. She rushes to the camp to warn her husband who already unknowingly sealed their son's fate.

Is it ironic that the Jewish boys of the settlement envied the impoverished Palestinians and snuck under the fence to play soccer with them while their parents cut off the Palestinians' water supply, steal their sheep, and demolish their homes? For this reason, making reparations is an expression of Interspiritual Judaism in solidarity with those experiencing injustice.

Story 2

In 2023, I attended a celebration for a bride and groom of Mexican and Palestinian descents. At the feast, my husband and I randomly joined people we had never met before: three Palestinians (American and Canadian) who emigrated 50 years ago and who have never been able to return to their villages, and a husband and wife from America, neither of whom were Jewish. In 2012, the husband of this couple went to the Hebron Hills, where my friend Awdah's village is located, to document an event supporting fair-trade olive farming communities in the Palestinian West Bank.

Interestingly, everyone at the table had been to the West Bank but me and my husband! At least I could tell my tablemates about my involvement with a handful of Jews in California and Quebec doing reparations for Palestinians in a village in *Masafer Yata*. While I wished I'd had the support of my local Jewish community as I told this story, I want to recognize the many international activists of all faiths working on behalf of occupied Palestinians as well as a small group of Jewish Israeli activists.

Our Jewish family must *listen and respond* to the spiritual activists among us. As American Jews, said Rabbi Burt, "*we recognize that our tax dollars support a right-wing Israeli government that is severely oppressing Palestinians. Israel's irresponsible actions have increased the level of antisemitism in the U.S. and around the world, which will inevitably affect our lives in this country.*"[79]

In addition to Israelis, the global Jewish community shares responsibility. Every *Yom Kippur* (the holy day of atonement), Jews declare that *we, as a community,* must make amends. Even if we cannot change things today, *we* must keep trying until we do. *Sumud.* So, I continue as a member of *Face to Face.*

While meeting via Zoom with Awdah in the summer of 2023, our group learned that things were getting worse. He told us, "*Soldiers support the settlers who use attack dogs on Palestinian women and children, point guns at us, prevent us from tending our crops or grazing our sheep. We villagers cannot afford animal feed so we must now sell our livestock.*" His hope was vanishing.

The next day, Awdah emailed us a photo of an order from the army – a document in Hebrew and Arabic stating that ten homes in his village would be destroyed within two weeks. One was his. It would not be the first time. And so, if Awdah requests donations for the villagers' legal fees to stop home demolitions in a court system designed to make them lose, is it worth it?

Over my lifetime, I'm glad to say our larger Jewish family has come a long way. We've listened better to those on the margin, and we do more to make them feel they belong. Today, we have rabbis who are women, gay, intermarried, colored, and trans and some who are anti-Zionist. We show the marginalized they're heard when, together, we innovate with our traditions so that everyone feels included and respected. The established Jewish community, however, remains stuck in terms of including those of us who have been standing up for Palestinian lives for decades. When will the mainstream Jewish community be ready to listen and change?

On July 28, 2025, Awdah Hathaleen, our Palestinian contact and friend, a human rights and peace activist, was shot and killed by an Israeli settler. He was 150 feet away. The settler was known.

Today, the village continues to be terrorized by Israeli soldiers and settlers while Awdah's killer walks free with impunity.

When Jews retreat to the traditional ethno-centric worldview, we fail to live up to the values of our tradition. In this retreat, we apply them only to our own members and act from a place of tribalism. At the same time, when we embrace a progressive worldview that denies our tradition, we may succeed in fighting for social justice for others but fail in our responsibility to our tribe. But, when Jews bring the tradition with us and welcome learning from others who welcome learning from us, then Judaism becomes something even better, a more mature version of itself. This may be true for all our tribes as they begin yearning to belong to the World.

Addendum:

I had ended this chapter by remembering Awdah's life as a blessing to us all, hoping we might gather -Jews and Palestinians- in the village of Umm al Kehir, at the Community Center of which he was so proud and had envisioned would one day be a tourist destination for peace. But as I write this now, the Israeli government plans to demolish all homes, agricultural facilities, and the beloved community center. If this goes forward, it will be a travesty and a tragedy that will haunt us all.

⑥
LOVING DUCKS

Peter Beinart, author of *Being Jewish After the Destruction of Gaza,* holds up a moral mirror to the Jewish community. Many Jews cannot or choose not to look into that mirror. Facing the cognitive dissonance that it would expose is too painful. Beinart's earlier blogs, from *before* October 7, can help us understand why.

On a trip to Israel in 2023 (*before* October 7), Beinart said, *"The first thing...I experience when I arrive in Israel is love...a sense of utter delight at being in a Jewish society."* Compared to living in the US, he says, which is like being a duck surrounded by horses, living in Israel is like being a duck among ducks. He continues,

> *You can thrive as a duck in [US] society. But it's still primarily a society of horses with norms and unstated assumptions that are horse-centric...that's kind of...what it's like to be a diaspora Jew even if you live on the Upper West Side of New York, like I do. And then you come [to Israel] ...surrounded by ducks of all different shapes and sizes...Some you find highly appealing. Some you don't find appealing...But they're all ducks, and the society is organized for ducks.* [80]

While it's enticing to live in a society where everyone is like you, there is a dark side. Such a society is like what Afrikaners created in S. Africa, Nazis in Germany, what white Christian Supremacists want for America and what Hindu Nationalists want for India. It is what extremist religious Israelis want for Israel. Beinart goes on to describe his divided self because he knows intellectually that equality for all of Israel's citizens and those living under military occupation would be the morally better society, but he loves to be a duck among ducks.

I understand Peter's divided self. It is why, in late 2021, I joined *Face to Face*, a Jewish Palestinian Reparations Alliance described earlier. Our group's goal is to listen, witness, provide financial aid, and advocate on behalf of a Palestinian village and for freedom and equality for all the land's inhabitants. When I first shared the work of F2F and sought donations, I lamented that not one Jewish friend asked me if they could join the group, yet some non-Jews did. A friend and trauma therapist explained why. She said I was like a baby unicorn among a flock of sheep, or, in this case, ducks.

This therapist understood collective Jewish trauma. She suggested I stop looking back expecting other Jews to follow this path. Instead, she suggested I focus on developing into a *confident unicorn*. But it's hard not to look back when you care and this is what Peter Beinart is sharing: the agony of *our* collective soul. I yearn to belong to a world where we all – ducks and horses, sheep and unicorns– live in peace. I want peace for Israelis and Palestinians. I want the ducks to come along. Is that so bad?

In Peter's next blog,[81] he invokes the Jewish holiday of *Tisha B'Av* (the 9th of Av), when Jews commemorate the destruction of the Temple (twice). He reminds us that *"the reason for the destruction of the Second Temple...is Sinat Chinam—baseless hatred, hatred among Jews."* With today's deep polarization among Jews (at least in America), it is not hard to wonder if such baseless hatred might cause Israel to fall again *in our times*.

Beinart goes on to say, *"One must recognize that Judaism is not simply a kind of individual spiritual or even moral pursuit. It is part and parcel of having obligations to other Jews."* According to the Talmud, a source of Jewish religious law, the antidote to baseless hatred is baseless love. Therefore, it behooves the Jewish people to love each other even when they disagree or find the behavior of other Jews to be morally wrong.

Beinart asks us to embrace the idea that,

> *We are to have more success in convincing other Jews that when we call for Palestinian freedom, and for historical justice for Palestinians, if we do so not from a position of indifference to the welfare of Jews, but from a place of love— indeed of baseless love.*

Progressive Jews in particular, he says, must love fellow Jews *unconditionally* if they hope to change their minds about Palestinians.

This baseless love explains why I look back, wait, and hope for my people to belong to something greater than our tribe. Baseless love is why my motto is *Belong to the World Bring Your Tribe*. Yet, even as Jews suffer from collective trauma (ancient and scarred, recent and raw), it is no excuse to kill innocent people. Such Israeli policies should push us to grow out of our ethno-centric worldview.

According to unicorn lore, unicorns represent all that is Good in the world and remind us to strive to be our best selves. For me, this means individuating from my tribe to chart a new path, a new form of Judaism untethered to political Zionism. This new form will operate from a consciousness of agency and activism.

Beinart describes activists like Jonathan Pollak as *"awe inspiring."* If there were more activists (unicorns?), apartheid in Israel might fall, he says. But Beinart admits he is not one of these activists. *"They're not being whipsawed like I am between... love of [Israeli] society and the hatred of the injustice that permeates it...And not just being enveloped in [this society] but loving its embrace."*

When we want to feel the embrace of our tribe, aren't we yearning to feel that we belong to something bigger?

What if the bigger thing wasn't our one tribe but all tribes? What if we evolve into seeing the world, even the cosmos, as that which holds us and to which we all feel we belong? What if we trusted

God? According to my therapist friend, if that trust could be restored, Jews and Palestinians might welcome belonging to a World that holds both. Together, we'd be a model for other tribes in other parts of the world struggling with similar conflicts.

Beinart dreams of *"a Jewish society integrated with a Palestinian society, having its own separate features but under conditions of equality and with some measure of historical justice."*[82] Sharing this vision is how we begin to remove the divided voice in our collective Jewish psyche. Instead, *"there would just be one."*

My friend is right; I need to develop confidence and courage to do what is morally right even if my tribe declares it taboo. We need to love our tribe but not just our tribe. To baselessly love only our tribe is to be stuck in ethno-centric thinking. We need a Judaism that opens itself to the world, with baseless love for all people. We need a new story of the world as our shared home, where all are sovereign and free. It's a world I want to live in and I'm willing to be a unicorn who does her best to love sheep, ducks, horses and others to help us get there. Isn't the point of our religions to help us try?

⑦
CAN BARBIE SAVE ISRAEL? PS AND THE US?

This essay is a parody of a parody. Analogies between today's Israel and Greta Gerwig's *Barbie* (2023) are admittedly broad strokes about diverse people (or dolls) in these real and fictional places. I am calling for a shift in consciousness to overcome denial, trauma, and cognitive dissonance through the practice of integration. Warning: *Barbie* spoilers.

As a preface, I am sharing an excerpt from Israeli writer and hostage negotiator, Gershon Baskin (Substack, July 21, 2025). He speaks to the dissonance in Israeli society, to which this essay alludes, when he says,

> There are so many positive things about Israeli society, but I fear our country is being overtaken by the ugly, the unjust, the criminal, the hate and the fear. Our society is violent – how can it not be when so many hundreds of thousands of us do what they do in Gaza and then come home living with post-trauma. Violent behavior, anger, frustration and guilt do not stop at the border when they come home. The dehumanization which is enlisted and enhanced in order to be able to commit the crimes that Israel is doing in Gaza and in the West Bank meet some kind of cognitive dissonance at home which finds justification for behaviors and actions that cannot ever be justified.

THE SLOGAN for Barbie the doll is "You Can Be Anything." The slogan for Israel the nation-state is "A Land without a People for a People without a Land." Both turn out to be untrue. Barbie Land and the State of Israel offer false utopias. But *Barbie* redeems its vision for girls. Can *Barbie* help Israel redeem its vision for Jews?

Barbie Land is for Women the way Israel is for Jews

In Barbie Land, Barbies delight in their all-girl world, chirping, *Hi, Barbie! Hi Barbie! Hi Barbie.* In Israel, Jews delight in their all-Jewish society, trading, *Shalom fellow Jew! Shalom fellow Jew!* In Barbie Land, dolls live a perfect life – *they can be and do anything* – but in the real world, girls cannot meet this ideal. Girls are miserable as they try to "be perfect".

In Israel, Jews live in a dreamy democracy for Jews only – *where they make the desert bloom*. But in the real world, they destroy villages and ethnically cleanse a whole people. Jews are miserable when they realize the actions of Israel do not match the idea of what it means to be Jewish.

When the fiction of fantasy and the facts of reality clash, an existential crisis is bound to erupt. This eruption starts with the breach between reality and vision.

Real World Meets Dream World

The original Barbie promises girls they can be judges, doctors, presidents, construction workers, and more. *They can be and do anything.* And they don't need a man's approval to be or do it. The original Israel promises all Jews the *right of return*, exerts regional power with nuclear arms, impresses the world as a *startup nation*, and more than marginalizes the Palestinian people. And they don't need the world's permission to do any of this.

In Barbie Land, Stereotypical Barbie (Margot Robbie) lives in an idyllic world on Malibu Beach where women run everything. The Barbies believe matriarchy in their dream world helps girls in the real world. But in the real world, women cannot *do and be anything*. They are not equal. Similarly, Israel oppresses and expels Palestinians believing this makes Jews in Israel and the Diaspora safer. But Israel's treatment of Palestinians not only hurts Palestinians, it also corrodes Israeli society and contributes to antisemitism around the world. Jews are less safe.

Stereotypical Barbie goes to the real world to reassure girls that the dream still works. Similarly, Zionists go to Congress to reassure Americans that Israel still works. But the damage is done.

Real World Punctures Dream World

Stereotypical Barbie suddenly thinks about mortality, wonders what it means to become a woman, and panics at the sight of fallen arches. Stereotypical Jews now question the morality of Israel, wonder what it means to be Jewish, and feel embarrassed by Israel's fallen image.

For many girls in the real world, and for many Jews outside of Israel, the moral injury of Barbie's failure and Israel's fall, respectively, run deep. Sasha (Ariana Greenblatt), the teenager in *Barbie*, no longer believes that Barbie represents her generation, if she ever did. The younger Jewish generation, especially in America, no longer believe that Zionism represents their generation, if it ever did.

Barbie changes Barbie Land to make life better in the real world. Can Israel learn from her example?

Cognitive Dissonance as Consciousness Raising

An existential crisis can be brought on by the discomfort of cognitive dissonance. This is also an opportunity for change and growth. It is the beginning of raising consciousness. In *Barbie*, an impromptu speech by Gloria (America Ferrera) reveals the existential crisis facing women in the real world: *"You have to never get old, never be rude, never show off, never be selfish, never fall down, never fail, never show fear, never get out of line. It's too hard! It's too contradictory!"*

The existential crisis facing Jews can be summed up this way: *You have to celebrate Israel's independence and never acknowledge the Nakba, you have to support a Jewish majority and never admit to the second class status of minorities, you have to accept Israel's military occupation and never punish settlers for pogroms they started or soldiers for demolishing homes or both for killing innocent people, you have to believe in the Jewish right of self-determination and never in Palestinians'. It's too hard! It's too contradictory!*

In Barbie Land, giving voice to the contradictions facing women breaks the spell of patriarchy. In the same way, if Jews articulate the cognitive dissonance they're experiencing today (as I hope I'm doing here), they can break the spell of Zionism. But what will replace it?

Barbie Land and Israel Re-Imagined

Once the spell of patriarchy is broken, Barbies do not, to their credit, reinstate the matriarchy. Stereotypical Barbie concedes, *"Not every night has to be girls' night."* Ken is encouraged to explore who he is rather than rely on Barbie for his self-worth. Nor does this new Barbie Land return to favoring Stereotypical Barbie over Weird Barbie, or Ken over Alan. These "misfits" (who helped take down *"Kendom"*) are now invited to share the power. Dare I compare Barbie's marginalized misfits (dolls played with too hard or too little) to Palestinians in Gaza, the West Bank, and Israel? Dare I suggest they are key to a true democracy for all and need to be invited to share power (not force)?

My 95-year-old mother, like many Jews of her generation, fears that giving Palestinians total equal rights will result in them taking over and kicking out the Jews. But *Barbie* shows us that *everybody is delusional*; neither matriarchy nor patriarchy will win out in the real world. Similarly, neither a Jewish-only democracy nor its emerging autocracy will succeed in the real world. Instead, *Barbie* invites us on a path to greater truth and humanity. This is what inspires people, plastic or real.

In the Barbie Land of greater truth and humanity, all Barbies are equal. In the real world, girls and women support this vision. (Mattel's limited edition of Weird Barbies flew off the shelf.) In an Israel-Palestine of greater truth and humanity, all Israelis and Palestinians can be equal. In the Interspiritual Age, Jews and Palestinians support this vision.

The Real Meaning of Becoming a Woman

Barbie is teaching girls what it *really* means to become a woman and to be proud of it. The message is that women are beautiful *no matter what changes* they go through. (Welcome, Ordinary Barbie! Welcome, Depressive Barbie!)

When it dawns on Barbie (Margot Robbie) that *to become a woman in the real world is to embrace change and mortality and that it doesn't have to be scary or bad,* she turns to the older woman (Ann Roth) sitting on the bench beside her and says, *"You're beautiful."* Roth smiles and laughs back, *"I know it."* There is beauty in change and joy in embracing it.

The Real Meaning of Being Jewish

Something similar can and is happening for Jews. Jews are realizing that what it means to be Jewish in relation to Israel is changing and it doesn't have to be scary or bad. Israel does not need to oppress Palestinians for Jews to practice their religion and culture. *Barbie*, the movie, challenges Jews to reform Israeli society where Jews and Palestinians enjoy equal rights, where divine sparks may grow separately but sparkle together.

There is beauty in embracing change that uplifts our spiritual and cultural traditions. This is true for all who identify with any religion(s) or ethnic group(s).

The women of Barbie Land learn that men also deserve to experience their lives with dignity. (The corollary is also true: Men learn that women deserve lives of equality and dignity.) So too can Jews in Israel learn that Palestinians deserve to experience their lives with dignity. (The corollary is also true: Palestinians understand that Jews deserve lives of security.) Everyone wins.

In saving Barbie Land, Barbie becomes a real woman. (And men can become real men.) In saving Israel, Israelis can become real Jews. (And Palestinians can become their real selves.) We must all encourage, entreat, and expect nothing less, not only for Israel, but for the United States as well.

PS Can *Barbie* Save the United States?

Barbie was released on July 21, 2023, ten weeks before October 7th. The events of that day, Israel's response to it, and the 2024 US presidential election outcomes fed a changing power dynamic around the globe. Instead of changing the minds of Israeli Jews, *Barbie* poked the sleeping bear of patriarchy in the United States and provoked a backlash to anyone or anything that might disturb its dream of ultimate power.

In addition to the soul of Israel, the soul of America needs saving. We might hope for a Judaism with new forms aligned to the consciousness of the Interspiritual Age. It's up to us to decide what kind of religion to celebrate and pass on, and then, *do it*.

In the *Barbie* movie, Barbie and Ken corrected their mistakes. The hope is that in real world, Israelis and Palestinians, Democrats and Republicans, as well Christians and Christians Nationalists correct theirs.

8

RABBIS IN A BAR

On a summer day in NYC, I arrived for my meeting at Jewish Theological Seminary, the rabbinic school for conservative rabbis. It was my first time in person at this larger-than-life institution that had occupied my youthful imagination. During my adolescence, I heard about JTS and longingly watched as male camp counselors whom I admired enrolled to become leaders in the Jewish community. On that warm day, I had arranged to meet with a Rabbi and teacher at the Seminary to discuss inter-religious education, but I secretly wondered if I only wanted a reason to step inside.

As I entered the building, my emotions caught me by surprise, and I wiped away trapped tears. I could not become a rabbi at JTS because first, I was female, but even when that barrier came down, I was barred for having married "out." (Today, the Reconstructionist denomination of Judaism allows rabbinic students to be intermarried but by then I had followed a different path.) Our Jewish leaders were obsessed with blaming intermarriage for its declining affiliation rates and a loss of Jews identifying with Judaism. But that prediction had not borne out.

"We no longer need to ask what might happen if we have significant numbers of Jews intermarrying, for this is already happening and we are seeing the result: These Jews—couples and families—are engaging with Judaism in beautiful, creative, meaningful ways," said Rabbi Denise Handlarski of Toronto, Ontario, a strongly conservative Jewish community.

While intermarriage correlated with declining rates of affiliation with Judaism, the establishment failed to see that this was a symptom, not a cause. Something else was going on.

Ever since, as a teenager, I stood in the synagogue parking lot observing with my friends that it was full and overflowing on only one day of the year (*Yom Kippur,* the holiest Jewish holiday), I knew something was off. What I saw as hypocrisy was present in other religions, too. Judaism was stuck. Both older and newer denominations such as Reconstructionism, Humanistic Judaism, Jewish Renewal, and even Traditional Egalitarian Orthodoxy were giving Jews options but all from the same dominant worldview (traditional and ethno-centric), one that faltered as modern and progressive worldviews emerged. Now, this worldview is wrangling to dominate from extreme nationalism. Paradoxically, traditional values can come forward without extremism, albeit through a world-centric worldview. It means letting go of the nationalism, the extremism, and opening to the new.

Some Jewish thought leaders have been thinking about what Judaism needs to thrive in the future. Here's a fictional story, Five Rabbis in a Bar, about what they may say.

FIVE RABBIS IN A BAR

Rabbis Strassfeld, Magid, Shapiro, Gottlieb, and Greenberg walk into a bar. It is the holiday, Lag B'Omer, the 33rd day between Passover and Shavuot. The bartender says to them, "If you can each tell me what Judaism needs to survive while standing on one foot,[83] I'll give you a free drink." (It's a Jewish bar.)

Rabbi Shapiro goes first, "Judaism will survive when Jews are blessings to all people of the world and appreciate the blessings others bring. The rest is commentary." The bartender nods and gives him a drink.

Rabbi Gottlieb, standing in tree pose, goes next. "Jews need to be *Shomrei Shalom* (keepers of peace) by following a Torah of Nonviolence, our prophetic tradition of social justice in allyship with all who struggle to be free of oppression." The bartender smiles and pours a drink.

Rabbi Strassfeld goes third. "Judaism needs to be permeable. It needs to let the outside world interact with it. It needs to demonstrate being a good worldly neighbor." The bartender winks and gives him a drink.

Rabbi Magid speaks next, standing on one foot, and says, "Judaism needs to reclaim exile as a positive Jewish experience, not as a bad thing. Being in exile keeps our tradition alive, even in Israel. To reclaim exile is to birth a future of peace between Israel and Palestine." The bartender grins and gives him a drink.

Rabbi Greenberg adds his voice, lifting one foot. "Judaism," he says, "is entering its Third Era and currently, God is hidden and self-limiting. This means the Jewish people need a new covenant with a hidden God." The bartender high-fives and pours a drink.

"Who is right?" ask the rabbis to the bartender.

The bartender replies, "Why don't you study the first half of Chapter 2 in the *Ethics of the Fathers (Pirkei Avot).*" The chapter states:

> He [Rabban Yohanan ben Zaqqai] said to [his disciples]: "Go forth [go out] and observe which is the right way [a path of integrity] to which a person should cleave." [Upon return] Rabbi Eliezer said, a good eye [to see others in a generous fashion]; Rabbi Joshua said, [to be] a good friend; Rabbi Yose said, [to be] a good neighbor; Rabbi Shimon said, to have

> foresight [to see that which is aborning: to be aware of consequences of one's actions; to see that which is just beginning to emerge]. Rabbi Elazar said, [to have] a good heart.

The five rabbis then debate over different ways to interpret this text. *What does it mean to cling to the right path? For how long and how far must one go forth? What should one observe? What does a good eye discern? What does it mean to be a good friend versus a good neighbor? What is being born on the margins that we should attend to and how? What does it mean to have a good heart? How does this apply to Jews today?*

As the rabbis cite sources from the Talmud and Mishnah, a thirsty child who was listening to all of this through an open window walks into the bar. Standing on one foot, the child says, "We should go forth with a new good heart."

What do you mean by "new," asked the rabbis who were all listening.

"An old good heart is open to our family. A new good heart is open to our family and all the other families of the world," said the child.

In the spirit of Rabbi Yohanan ben Zaqqai, the bartender quoted the last verse of Chapter 2, *"Rabban Yohanan] said to them [his disciples]: In the words of Elazar ben Arakh [who answered, a 'good heart'], I see your words, for in Elazar's words, all of your words are included."*

In unison, the rabbis chant, "Give this kid a drink!"

PS It's a non-alcoholic bar.

⑨
LEADERS, TEACHERS, HEALERS

A clash between faculty and students at a rabbinic college over its requirement to study in Israel reflects the growing schism in the Jewish community at large. This one year requirement was shortened to one semester but for anti-Zionist students, no time in the current Zionist state is acceptable.[84] It should be no surprise that a younger generation of Americans is more sympathetic to Palestinians than to Israelis.[85]

When I spoke with friends over age 65, all sided with the college. One said, *"I don't get how Zionism has become a dirty word. It makes me sad to think that people who are becoming rabbis won't go to Israel. That's Nutty!"* Another suggested the students join activist groups working with Israelis and Palestinians while fulfilling the program's requirement. These views represent a generational divide; the older generation having bought into Israelism and the younger rejecting it.

For the younger generation, it is not about *how* the students show up but where they draw moral lines. To insist on studying in Israel *today* goes against their belief that any time or money spent in Israel supports occupation, displacement, and erasure of an entire people.

The argument that studying in Israel is a requirement to become a Rabbi belongs to ethno-centric thinking at best and Israel-centric thinking at worst. For the Interspiritual Age, we need integral thinking. Not only must we change the way we celebrate and teach Judaism but also the way we train future Jewish leaders - rabbis, teachers, and healers.

Requiring rabbinic students to study in Israel may no longer be necessary. Judaism can free itself of political Zionism to create something better. As a new Jewish community emerges, one which embraces interspiritual solidarity, the Jewish community in Israel and in the diaspora can get unstuck.[86]

What would a rabbinic and teachers program look like in the Interspiritual Age?

I imagine rabbinic students would study in *different* Jewish *and other religious* communities around the world. They'd explore and create connections between members of Jewish communities and others. In doing so, these future leaders will form friendships. Friendships will be key to the inter-religious programs that follow. Indeed, the *Global House of Friendship and Hope,* run by the Elijah Interfaith Institute, encourages religious leaders to meet regularly and offers guidelines for committing to and practicing friendship.

The rabbinic program I envision includes friendships within Judaism and across faiths. It celebrates accomplishments of Jewish communities not only in Israel but *around the globe.* The land between the river and the sea may be special to Jews and to Palestinians, but that does not diminish other places where Jews or Palestinians live.

An Interspiritual Jewish rabbinic program could include interfaith experiences (dialogue and exegesis) as well as inter-religious peace building. Students could study for Jewish *smicha* (ordination) and for a "minor *smicha*" in another religion, training with those spiritual leader(s). Jewish rabbinic programs could also offer a *minor smicha* to spiritual leaders of other religions. Judaism in the Interspiritual Age will welcome rabbis who are dual or triple ordained. This is not a stretch. There are already rabbis with training in other religions, particularly Buddhism.[87] The difference is, it would now be the norm.

In the Interspiritual Age, rabbis interested in pastoral care or spiritual healing will receive training in Jewish intergenerational trauma. Science shows that the trauma of the Holocaust in the collective Jewish psyche is passed down through generations. The work of Rabbi Tirzah Firestone[88] as well as Gabor Mate and Thomas Hubl provide inspiration for doing so.

In addition to therapy, psychedelics might become a healing modality. In March of 2025, Harvard Law School hosted a symposium with over 700 attendees on *Psychedelics in Monotheistic Traditions: Sacramental Practice and Legal Recognition*. Rabbis interested in pastoral care could become certified in psychedelics as a tool for helping some people heal from historical collective trauma. In a recently published study on clergy and psychedelics, researchers found,

> *Most gave 'strong or extreme endorsement' that the experience 'increased their effectiveness in their religious vocation' (79%) and 'increased the sense of the sacred in daily life (79%).*

One of the architects of the study said, "*It could pave the way for some very constructive things in the future in medicine, education and religion.*"[89]

One advocate for legalizing psychedelics said,

> *I've always felt that the response to the Holocaust is helping people realize our common humanity... psychedelic mystical experiences are one of the ways... I felt like what I'm doing is to try to prevent another Holocaust...* [90]

The evolution of consciousness involves spiritual growth. Because religion, a domain of spirituality, holds so much sway over our worldviews, religious leaders in Judaism -rabbis and educators- are in a privileged position to help us learn and grow. In the Interspiritual Age, religious schoolteachers will also have experience in other religions and training in how to teach religion, with philosophy, for children. It will be the norm (not the exception) for teachers of Judaism to join others in immersive programs of religious literacy and interfaith education.[91]

To be clear, Interspiritual Judaism is not about bringing the world to the tribe but the tribe to the world. The recent trend in Jewish education to bring children into an immersive study of modern Hebrew through charter schools is one example of this misuse and perhaps abuse. The goal of the Hebrew Language Academy (HLA), a public charter school program with locations in ten states *so far*, is to teach Hebrew to children of all backgrounds along with a love for the state of Israel. HLA claims that, *"Students learn with native Hebrew-speaking teachers about Israel's culture and history. These areas of study culminate in an 8th-grade Capstone trip to Israel."* [92]

In the HLA model, children of all backgrounds are welcome and are exposed to another language (and why not Hebrew) but no other languages are offered and the cultivation of child ambassadors for a state that some claim is committing genocide seems more like a public relations strategy than a beneficial byproduct.[93] When I shared this story with a friend, she asked rhetorically, *"Can you imagine if public charter schools in America taught Arabic and love for a Palestinian state?"*

There may be good things about HLA but next to The Interspiritual Classroom, its model is exclusive, ethno-centric, attached to political Zionism (both Israeli and Christian), and aligned with Israel's procedural (not liberal) democracy. Instead of *Belong to the World Bring your Tribe,* HLA reflects *Belong to your Tribe Bring the World.* It turns the evolution of consciousness inside out and substitutes tribalism for global citizenship. *Is this what we want?*

In the Interspiritual Age, Jewish educators will teach Judaism in a way that is nondual, integral, inclusive, detached from nationalistic Jewish and Christian Zionism, aligned with liberal democracy and open to learning from and alongside other religions. For years I explored teaching this form of Judaism with a small group of students from Jewish and Jewish-Interfaith families. Parents wanted a way to celebrate Judaism with their families and institutional forms of Judaism at the time had little appeal. Today, a growing number of Jewish parents are unwilling to embrace Jewish ethnonationalism as the center of their children's identity.

We now see "Diasporist" Jewish religious schools (like *Achvat Olam* in Boston) proudly announce their program as an "alternative, rooted in Diasporism" as opposed to Israelism. Diaspora-centric Judaism is an antithesis to Israel-centric Judaism and may be a necessary steppingstone to outgrow the latter. But this dialectic is incomplete. A world-centric Judaism that can hold a new form of Judaism for Jews in Israel *and* in the Diaspora culminates in the synthesis of what I call Interspiritual Judaism.

Evolving into this synthesis may happen in its own time. It may be interrupted by more powerful forces working against it. It may receive help from the "evolutionaries" concerned with the survival of humanity and its multifaceted culture.

The table below offers a few ideas for how evolutionaries in roles of leaders, teachers and healers can contribute to systemic change in bringing our tribes to the integrative consciousness of the Interspiritual Age.

Of course, there are additional roles people can fill to help manifest of the vision of Interspiritual Judaism. These include program coordinators who can influence the type of programs offered to congregational and non-congregational members of religious communities. I want to give a shout out to Marie Pattipati, Cultural Arts and Education director at the Jewish Community Center in Ann Arbor, Michigan, for putting energy into curating a Hanukkah-Diwali community wide event. It was also encouraging to see that a student in Jewish leadership program served to help make the program a success. If she goes on to become a leader in a Jewish institution, I will be encouraged by the multicultural programs that could be coming.

As our values widen and deepen to reflect the growing integral consciousness of the Interspiritual Age, we will see more programs that bring people of different faith backgrounds together.

Suggestions for Religious Congregations, Schools, and Communities

Leaders	Teachers	Healers
clergy, community program developers, funders, campus ministries, nonprofit and seminary directors	*private day and after schoolteachers, K-12, teachers of teaching programs (trainers)*	*therapists, facilitators, restorative justice practitioners, truth and reconciliation healers, spiritual activists*
develop friendships with clerics in other religions	develop friendships with teachers of other religions	develop friendships with healers of other faiths
build coalitions with other faith communities	integrate interfaith and interspiritual lessons into the curriculum	offer ongoing workshops for healing inherited collective trauma for a religious community
design surveys that measure integrity and validate interspiritual identity	take students on tours of other worship places	offer ongoing workshops for members of different communities to share collective trauma healing
invite another cleric to give a guest sermon, and offer to give one to their congregation	visit other religious school classrooms and be visited	
include interfaith and interspiritual courses in seminaries, and offer secondary ordinations	invite guest teachers and be invited	institute opportunities for reparations within and between communities
	train future teachers to integrate interfaith education in lessons	show up in solidarity for other groups and be shown up for
encourage students in communal leadership programs to network with other students in theirs	coordinate with leaders and healers when developing new programs	share your work with the leaders and teachers

⑩

POST-TRIBAL JUDAISM, INTERSPIRITUAL HUMANITY

In 2018, Michael Chabon, an American novelist, short story writer, screenwriter, and columnist, said that intermarriage of all types is *"the source of all human greatness,"* and then added, *"Any religion that relies on compulsory endogamy to survive has, in my view, ceased to make the case for its continued validity in the everyday lives of human beings."*[94] An astounding statement for in-married Jews to hear. For intermarried Jews, not so much.

Many years before Chabon's statement, a Jewish intermarried neighbor and I stood on our sidewalk lamenting and *keveling*. Our conversation went something like this:

Richard: Why are so many Jews against intermarriage? We're spreading knowledge of Judaism through our spouse's families. It's a good thing.

Me: I agree. My spouse's family learns about Judaism from me and I learn about them, in terms of religion. It doesn't make me less Jewish.

Richard: Our kids feel comfortable learning about Judaism and learning about the other members of their extended family.

Me: The Jewish establishment thinks we're destroying Judaism, but maybe we're saving it.

Richard: Ironically, interfaith marriage will save Jews from a neo-Nazi resurgence. Many people wouldn't know any Jews without intermarriage.

Me: One day, they'll thank us for making Jews safer, not less.

Interfaith marriages have allowed families to explore new and multiple ways of belonging. Instead of identifying with a single religion, these family members are comfortable with "multiple belonging." Chabon's statement is the flip side of Teilhard de Chardin's prediction that if religions are to survive, they must be Interspiritual.

Interfaith marriages are one way of evolving towards interspiritual humanity. To survive, each religion must evolve from tribalism to get there. If our religious tribes remain stuck in ethno-centric, mythical-magical thinking run amok (nationalism turned into supremacy), we will fail to include and transcend, i.e., to evolve.

Transcending tribal thinking requires a new vision. Just as Civil War abolitionists needed a new vision of freedom (reflective as opposed to atomic) *before* the tide of public sentiment burst in their favor, today, world-centric thinkers need a new vision of religion (interspiritual as opposed to ethno-centric) before the tide of public sentiment swells in its favor.

In the spirit of political economist Albert O. Hirschman's 1970 volume, *Exit, Voice, and Loyalty,* a seminal book about options for organizations in decline (such as religion), it is not enough to leave (Exit), to protest (give Voice), to wait for things to get better (neglectful Loyalty) or pretend all is well (optimistic Loyalty).[95] For our religions to reach the Interspiritual Age, we need new forms, new institutions. If we leave a religion in decline, without a strategy, we cede the space to extremists. If we protest without listening to others' grievances, we miss opportunities for growth. If we are uncritically loyal, we risk losing everything.

Fortunately, Jews and Palestinians who realize they need each other for liberation are forming solidarity movements. Groups like Jewish Voice for Peace, If Not Now, Center for Jewish Non-Violence, and others, call for collective liberation. In this process, we must be attentive to those who worry that their identity will be lost. *How will we maintain our religion's individual integrity?*

Like a good neighbor, we will help our religious partners in ways which they ask us, without imposing our will. I know this is possibly from the Face to Face Alliance I've experienced. We also know from true stories of interfaith examples of solidarity. In 2011, for example, in Alexandria, Egypt, Christian Copts formed a protective human shield around Muslims as they prayed in the public square, and Muslims formed a "human shield" around churches at Christmas after an attack on Copts. We know it from the Muslim family in Kolkata, India that cares for three empty synagogues so they will be in good shape for whenever a Jewish community returns.[96] We know it from an Indigenous Council inviting a synagogue to help protect their lands. We know it from Black-Jewish coalitions supporting their church and synagogue members to get to know each other. We have and we can show up for each other.

As our religions move to post-tribalism, mystical teachings and interfaith dialogue can become the norm. We can celebrate each other's differences from a place of unity. This is what nondualism teaches: *to see the uniqueness in each one as a manifestation of the Oneness that is all of us.* Rabbis, pastors, imams, ministers, swamis, medicine men/women, etc., clerics of all religions, joining together.

In *The Jew in the Lotus*, Roger Kamenetz, a journalist, was invited to observe a group of distinguished rabbis traveling to meet the Dalai Lama. The Dalai Lama invited them to share Jewish wisdom on how to survive in Exile so he could help his exiled people in Tibet. (Remember, Exile and Return is Judaism's special gift.) The rabbis were excited about the trip and couldn't stop talking about their great ideas for the Dalai Lama. At one point, the organizing rabbi interrupted and admonished them. *Don't you know why you are on this trip? It is not only to teach His Holiness, but to learn from Him. You must come with an openness to learning.*[97]

If we approach teaching and learning each other's religions from an attitude of epistemic humility (recognizing our own understanding as limited), we will find wholeness through interspiritual community. As McIntosh notes, this wholeness may be expressed through a philosophy of spirituality that unites the arts, sciences, humanities, and religions.[98] This wholeness may be the very purpose of our human evolution. A post-tribal Jewish community and shared interspiritual humanity is one I would like to embrace and that I would like to embrace me.

③

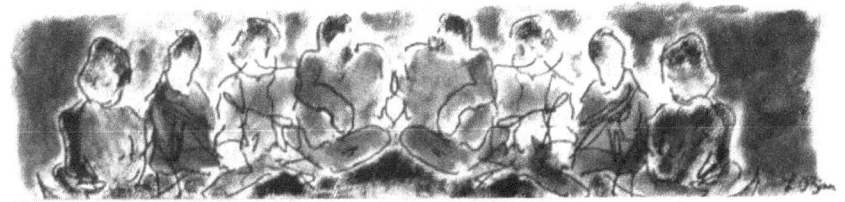

PART THREE

BECOME INTERSPIRITUALLY JEWISH

Matt, the Jewish father in an interfaith family with two young girls, shared this story: Matt's mother (the girls' Jewish grandmother) asked if he would raise the girls Jewish. "Yes," he said, "but it won't look like the Jewish that *I* was raised with, or the Jewish *you* were raised with. It will look like the Jewish *they* will be raised with."

What will it look like?

In *Tablets Shattered*, Joshua Leifer expresses the challenge this way:

> *Non-orthodox American Judaism faces a profound, fundamental crisis of content and purpose...Having outsourced nearly all its content to Israel, American Jewish life can no more evade Israel and Zionism than choose to dissolve. If it doesn't find a new foundation on which to stand, it might anyway collapse.* (p.229)

If Leifer's right, we need a new foundation. But it won't come as an alternative within the same consciousness of our legacy forms of Judaism. Today, we need models and examples of teaching and doing religion that lay the foundation for new, interspiritual forms of Judaism (or new interspiritual forms for your religion, if it's in decline).

As I've tried to show, the new form values "integrity and connection" over "identity and continuity." It requires growth in consciousness and educational models to support it. Interspiritual Judaism is the natural, evolutionary development that allows us to experience Judaism anew. To review, we might describe it as nondual, universal, integral, inclusive, detached from political Zionism, supportive of integral consciousness, aligned with liberal democracy, and open to learning alongside other religions.

Nondual

Nondual Judaism values the mystical teachings of Judaism. One reason why many of today's Jewish baby boomers fled Judaism in the 70's and 80's for Eastern or Hasidic communities was because they were looking for mystical teachings. One of my principles (or value-tensions) in teaching Judaism in The Interspiritual Classroom is to design lessons with Jewish mysticism *(Kabbalah)* in age-appropriate ways. Another is to integrate (not blend, syncretize, appropriate or assimilate) teachings from other religions but to show respect and appreciation for shared values. It also includes opening to other religions so they too can learn appropriately from us.

Who knows what? And about whom do they know it?

Pew Research found that,

> *Compared with other Americans, U.S. Jews have relatively high levels of religious knowledge – including about non-Jewish religions like Christianity, Islam and Sikhism. But most non-Jewish Americans are unable to answer some basic factual questions about Jewish practices, including about the Jewish Sabbath and New Year.*[99]

These results indicate that Jews need to open more to others about their religion but also to change within their religion. Some Jews do not learn about how their teachings are influenced by the culture at large which includes influence from other religions. Jay Michelson notes that the Hebrew expression, *Ein Od Milvado*

(There is Nothing Besides Him) really means there is nothing but God. God is all that is. God is existence itself. As Rami Shapiro puts it, there is nothing but God Godding. While this saying appears on bumper stickers in Israel, the issue is not that it's made its way into pop culture, but what we do with the idea of a nondual God.

Universal
Judaism in the Interspiritual Age opens us to universal teachings of all religions. It is in the arena of shared mysticism that common values for working together are found. Differences among religions are honored and celebrated. As Gottlieb teaches, we don't appropriate another's culture or ritual without their permission. But why would we want to when, in the Interspiritual Age, we can experience it with them during occasions of shared celebration.

Integral
Integral refers to what evolutionary philosophers like Ken Wilber call the next stage of consciousness. It follows the post-modern worldview. With integral consciousness taking root, we will see more harmonization in all sectors of society and solutions to the problems that progressivism failed to adequately address (due to an inability to create political solidarity for advancing progressive ideas).

Inclusive
According to the authors of *Counting Inconsistencies*,

> *At a minimum, more than 20 percent of 'Jewish households' include people who identify as nonwhite. If the population trends along the same lines as the U.S. Census, then some decades from now Jews of Color will become the majority of U.S. Jews.*[101]

Ashkenazi-centric Jewish leaders who function within this ethno-centric worldview have a hard time making Jews of Color feel included. But from a world-centric worldview, everyone can feel included. Inclusion can be lifted into belonging. Rabbi Jonathan Sacks (z'l) wrote,

> *We make a mistake when we think religion is only about believing. It's also about belonging; and belonging is about community, that delicate yet powerful network of relationships where we learn moral literacy-by being there for other people when they need us, knowing that they'll be there for us when we need them.* [100]

The vision for Interspiritual Judaism supports the kind of mutual aid and community caring that Sacks describes.

Detached from political Zionism
Interspiritual Judaism is uncoupled from political Zionism. Political Zionism turned a homeland into a nation-state needing a Jewish majority to sustain its Jewish identity. This meant more civil rights for Jews than for non-Jews. This is antithetical to democracy and the spirit of Judaism where all people deserve to be treated with dignity. Israel's military occupation of Palestinians does not reflect Interspiritual Judaism.

While Zionism claims holiness in a piece of land, Judaism claims holiness in a piece and peace of time. As Rabbi Abraham Joshua Heschel states in *The Sabbath,* God created the world in six days and on the seventh God did NOT declare a holy site where He was to be worshiped; God declared a holy time: the sabbath. On the 7th day God created *rest* and made *the day* holy. Only later did King David, not God, plan to build a Temple in Jerusalem. The land will always be special for Jews *and* for Palestinians. Not only does this land not belong to anyone, no land belongs to anyone. According to Torah, *"But the land must not be sold beyond reclaim, for the land is Mine; you are but strangers resident with Me."* (Leviticus 25:23).

To consider Judaism untethered to Zionism is a growing idea. Today, Jews can take a course on *Judaism Beyond Nationalism* (American Council for Judaism). In it, Rabbi Shaul Magid talks about post-ethnic Judaism in America, the growing crisis of Zionism, and reimagining Jewish life beyond nationalism. Professor Atalia Omer talks about Judaism through social justice, post-Zionism, solidarity with Palestinians, and ritual innovation. The ideas in this book have good company.

Supporting Interspirituality

Interspiritual, Integral, or World-centric Judaism are terms for the new Judaism emerging today. The work of Rabbi Lynn Gottlieb for Judaism based on the Torah of nonviolence is also aligned with this worldview. While it may be difficult for people who built their identity around the political Zionist ideology to transcend it, I believe they will find a richer and deeper Judaism in doing so. More importantly, Judaism, detached from political Zionism, will attract the next generation. For and with them, we reimagine Judaism today.

For Judaism to flourish, Jews around the world might share their experiences of faith, community, and identity with Jews in -for example- Jerusalem, Mexico, India, or Uganda (intrafaith) AND with Muslims in Jakarta, Christians in Atlanta, and Bedouins in Umm al-Khair (interfaith). We have the technology to do so. We only need the imagination to make it happen.

Learning Alongside and From Other Religions

If Religion Educators have models, examples, and stories of how to celebrate holidays, explore spirituality, and teach religion from an interfaith and interspiritual context, then they can design lessons and programs to advance the evolution of consciousness in our culture.

For Rabbi Rami Shapiro, a simple standard for evaluating the programs we design and implement is: *Are we blessings for all the peoples of the earth?*[102] For philosopher Steve McIntosh, we evaluate if our spiritual teachings bear fruit: *"Do they vanquish fear and promote compassion? Do they increase morality and loving-kindness?"*[103] When we ask new questions of old material, we move beyond the methods of a previous paradigm, changing the "map" from which new research and learning flows. Science then evolves from one paradigm to the next.[104] Culture evolves similarly from one stage of consciousness to the next. New questions yield new insights into our and other religions' teachings. Such a paradigm shift changes the map.

PART THREE presents familiar landmarks -holidays- on the road to a new vision for Judaism, one that aligns with the Interspiritual Age. While I could focus on other aspects of Judaism, holidays are accessible and familiar to most. As such, they provide a map for traveling through the Jewish year. With this map, we can imagine Judaism in the Interspiritual Age and become interspiritually Jewish.

These are only beginning ideas, early steps in our interspiritual evolution of embracing such core spiritual values as peace, truth and transcendence - values that come from recognizing the divine in ourselves and in others. As people from all traditions add their practical ideas for bringing us closer to the maturation of our religions in the Interspiritual Age, more of its worldview will manifest.

When Wells Fargo Advisors Managing Director, Yakub Mathew, invited people from different faiths to join him on a once-in-a-lifetime quest to Maha Kumbh Mela (the world's largest religious gathering and Hindu pilgrimage), he found shared humanity beyond faith divisions. Fifty living thought leaders added their voices to the experience captured in his book, *Seeking the Infinite: Maha Kumbh 2025*. Mathew's heartfelt plea for interspirituality in practice comes through when he says,

> *So many great religions have been created to create better people...But in the end, it has become a source of control of resources, a source of power, and that has created, 'My religion is better than your religion.' The deaths and havoc organized religion has created is worse than anything imaginable as far as wars and other things which have happened. Which religion says killing people is good? None, but it has resulted in that. So when you see all these things, all one can say is that one must be able to either use religion to become spiritual, or one must be spiritual to enhance one's journey — to be tolerant, realized and conscious. One must not be divisive.* [118]

Sharing humanity's common heritage of spiritual wisdom across traditions for an experience of oneness and unity, of infinity within, is more valuable than the experience of separation and divisiveness our religions hold onto. May the following ideas of celebrating Jewish holidays bring us closer to a new vision for Judaism and for all religions. As for teaching religion in the Interspiritual Age, that is the subject of the next book.

①
HANUKKAH AND HEGEL

You've heard of Hegel, the German idealist (1770-1831) known for his *dialectic* philosophy? (Go ahead. Say it. dīəˈlektik. It's fun.) Because Hegel's philosophy underlies the integral or interspiritual worldview, we can ask: *How can Hegel help us interpret Hanukkah for the Interspiritual Age? How can Hanukkah help us make sense of Hegel?*

If we think of each night of Hanukkah as an expansion of consciousness in the spiritual evolution of culture, we can begin to make sense of Hegel and celebrate Hanukkah in its fullness. But first, some background. Hegel's discovery of the dialectic is to history what Watson-Crick-Franklins' discovery of the double-helix is to science. DNA is the code for our biological evolution, but the dialectic drives our personal, social and cultural evolution. Both are depicted in the shape of a spiral.

How does it work?
Thesis, antithesis, and synthesis. OR identity, polarity difference, and identity-and-difference as a new identity. When opposing dual perceptions (thesis and antithesis) come into conflict, parts of each are preserved and negated, and then synthesized into something new, the next thesis.

This continuous, recapitulating spiral of "including and transcending" what came before allows for the growth of consciousness. Hegel tapped into the evolutionary method of the universe that moves us through our own lives, from one worldview to the next. Each passage, through a new layer of consciousness, reveals different and deepening values. Each produces a clash of views propelling us to new ways of thinking about the world.

Based on Hegel's *Phenomenology of Spirit/Mind* and the work of integral philosophers who came after him, we can summarize each stage of consciousness with each candle of the *Chanukkiah* (the eight branched *menorah*). I will spare you from Hegel's abstruse language and offer more palatable descriptions of each stage, per philosopher Steve McIntosh (*Integral Consciousness*) minus the tensions that give rise to subsequent stages of consciousness. These descriptions are to be read as we light each of the eight candles.[105] As is part of our Jewish tradition, we also say the blessings that accompany this holiday.

The 1st candle, lit on the first night, is for neonatal survival, and "awareness" as *Archaic Consciousness*.

The 2nd candle/night is for *Tribal Consciousness* inspiring loyalty to family and ancestors.

The 3rd candle/night is for *Warrior Consciousness*, the fire to express power, to develop an ego or self.

The 4th candle/night is for *Traditional Consciousness*, the shift from an ego-centric to an ethno-centric morality; a shared belief system that values law and order as well as honesty.

The 5th candle/night is for *Modern Consciousness,* the Age of Enlightenment, reason and science, freedom and democracy; progress.

The 6th candle/night is for *Postmodern Consciousness*, a world-centric morality of responsibility to all others.

The 7th candle/night is for *Integral Consciousness* (the Interspiritual Age or World-centric with a capital W) that integrates all religious and spiritual paths, harmonizes science and religion, and links personal with social evolution.

The 8th candle/night is for *Post-Integral Consciousness and* continues the gradual perfection of humanity through the development of the primary values of Goodness, Truth, Beauty.

Gaze into the light. Breathe deeply. Take in the idea of the growth of consciousness, the spiral of humanity's evolution.

Nowhere do we need this more than in the way we use or don't use religion. Even the rabbis of old, when they saw the extremism in the nationalistic tendencies of the Maccabees, countered it. They shifted the celebration away from tribalism and its focus on military victory and to the rededication of our faith by giving us the story of the miracle of light. They taught that Hanukkah was to be celebrated for the miracle of the little cruz of oil that burned for eight days when the Maccabees cleaned up the Temple. With Hanukkah, we rededicate ours lives to Judaism, to spiritual values, and to being the light, raising the light, and helping others shine.

By lighting the way of our spiritual evolution from one candle to the next, we can interpret the holiday as honoring the old stories, our history, our ancestors and creating new ones that are relevant to our times and our descendants. Perhaps today the miracle is not so much what the light stands for as much as how we gather to stand in it.

Cautionary Notes:

1. We go through stages of consciousness individually and collectively. We can grow at any time.

2. The stages are not deterministic. They describe a pattern and they continue indefinitely.

3. Appreciation for Hegel's philosophy, ourselves and our universe, may increase with the consumption of latkes.

② INTERSPIRITUAL HANUKKAH

I'll demonstrate how we can fast track to the Interspiritual Age with Jewish holidays by celebrating the holiday of Hanukkah in three steps. This chapter serves as a script you can use with your family or community to celebrate this holiday in a way that helps move us from one worldview to the next. Here's your script:

Welcome Everyone! Thank you for joining an Interspiritual Hanukkah Holiday Lights Party where we are *zipping to an interspiritual age.*

According to *Belong to the World Bring your Tribe*, our human culture is due for a paradigm shift. The shift we need to make is from the postmodern age to the interspiritual age. So, here's the question:

How can we celebrate *Hanukkah* from the worldview of the Interspiritual Age?

We will learn through a 3-Step journey that takes us and Hanukkah from the mono-faith age (Separation) to the interfaith age (Recognition), to the Interspiritual Age (Reunion or Integration).

STEP 1: Hanukkah in the Mono-faith Age

The Old Story...SEPARATION

Setting: Pick a room for this step. Decorate accordingly.

Step One is right now, right here, in this space where the Hanukkah menorah is displayed in a window. Let me tell you about the Old Story behind it. The year is 165 BCE; the place is Judea. The people are Jewish. The government is Seleucid Syrian Greek (due to Alexander the Great's conquest) and the dominant culture is Greek Hellenism.

The Jews are arguing (what's new?) about how to be Jewish in a Greek culture, about how much Greek is too much Greek.[106] Sound familiar? The ruler, Antiochus IV, decides for them. He bans the practice of Judaism. He sends an army, kills people, and desecrates the Temple. The Jews fight back, led by the Maccabee family, and two years later, they win. When they clean up the Temple, they find a little bit of olive oil to light the menorah in the Temple and rededicate their lives to Jewish values. The light miraculously lasts for eight days. Thus, the holiday lasts that long.

The monofaith tradition of lighting the menorah each night for eight nights reminds us to: 1) value our religious freedom and the right to be different, and 2) rededicate ourselves to Judaism.

The message is: We must defend our differences. We do things that keep us separate from others to maintain our differences or we won't survive. Some Jews sum up the holiday as *"they tried to kill us. We won. Let's eat."*

Monofaith is the story that happens in the Age of Separation, differentiating from Others, a brilliant survival strategy for that time. When we light the menorah and tell this story, we reinforce that separation. To experience the monofaith story, we sing the traditional blessings. *(Be ready to provide paper or digital copies of the Hanukkah blessings to participants. Sing them together.)* And let us say: Happy Hanukkah!

If it's a Friday night, we also welcome the Sabbath, a sacred time of rest and renewal, prayer and re-union with God, community, family, and our innermost being. *(Provide Shabbat blessings to recite. Have your candles, wine, and challah ready.)* This too follows the story of Separation, separating the holy from mundane. Embracing this sacred time, we say: Shabbat Shalom! (If it's a Saturday night, be ready to add the blessings of Havdalah.)

Remember! You're on a journey. Separation is one stop. Enjoy it with dinner and each other's company. *(Have latkes ready!)* Then go to Step 2.

STEP 2: Hanukkah in the Age of Interfaith

The Middle Story...RECOGNITION

So here we are in a different room where you see a Christmas tree or symbol of the local dominant religion. Since Christianity is the predominant religion in America where this example takes place, a Christmas tree is apropos. The great thing about intermarriage is that it forces holidays to interact; it's not optional. So, Step 2 in our 3-step journey centers around interfaith dialogue. It's the middle story. It's what happens when Hanukkah and Christmas (or any two or more different faith traditions) get together. It reflects some of what we call assimilation, another brilliant ancestral survival strategy, and also self-determination in that Jews get to be Jews.

Interfaith dialogue with Christianity, as an example, might go as follows. *(Use props such as a Santa hat and a dreidel, or have different people for each part, to indicate the different roles.)*

Christmas: Hey, Hanukkah, what's happening?

Hanukkah: Hey Christmas, I've got eight candles burning; I'm hot tonight!

Christmas: Hey, you know, we have candles, too.

Hanukkah: Really? I just see electric lights.

Christmas: Well, it's called Advent, the four weeks leading up to me. We light four different candles on a wreath, often for a different theme each week. Themes are Hope, Love, Peace, and Joy. It shows the growing brightness of Jesus' coming.

Hanukkah: Interesting! In my tradition, the rabbis debated whether to start with eight candles and decrease by one each night or start with one and increase each night up to eight.[107] They chose to increase because it gave more hope during the dark days.

This mini dialogue is a precursor to enriching and expanding experiences that can result from interfaith engagement. Through dialogue, if we are willing, we learn about the Other. And the more we learn, the more we see common values between the different, separate holidays and their people.

> *This kind of experience is beginning to appear in mainstream religious spaces. One Jewish community held a celebration of Hanukkah (Judaism), Diwali (the Hindu festival of light), and Sigd (a holiday of Ethiopian Jewry) for two years in a row. The event planners included foods of each culture, children's involvement in rituals, and adults and children sharing each other's cultural dances. Kudos to the planners! I look forward to more programs like this one with other religions exploring other themes and hope the next step, Reunion/Integration, follows.*

The Interfaith Age is a story of Recognition, of recognizing oneself in the Other. We all have similar elements in our traditions. If the Mono-faith Age is the story of Separation, of forming a separate identity from others, then the Interfaith Age is the story of recognizing, of knowing and being known by the Other. This is why interfaith dialogue is so important AND why separation must precede it. There won't be anyone there to recognize if we have not separated first. In this act, no single tradition needs to be replaced. My mentor, Rabbi Joseph H. Gelberman used to quip, "Always in addition to, never instead of." We can invite learning from and alongside other religions into our celebrations to generate the social and spiritual solidarity needed today.

Let's continue our journey. Where does Recognition lead next?

STEP 3: Hanukkah in the Interspiritual Age

The New Story...REUNION (aka Integration)

How about those latkes?! *Thanks to all you great chefs!* Why do we consume oil? Because the old story says: a little bit of oil lasted longer than expected. A miracle!

In fact, the rabbis invented that story 250 years after the event to tamp down the popular nationalism associated with Hanukkah and to limit the power of the "illegal" Hasmonean priests.[108] (This invention also explains the discrepancy between the Hanukkah menorah's 9 branches and the Temple's 7. The eight-day holiday is based on copying the eight days of Passover and of Sukkot, not on a miracle.)

Hanukkah reveals the tension between the desire for political independence (Maccabean then and more recently, Zionism) and a religious practice based on the study of Torah and lately, of Talmud. Both desires reflect the Monofaith Age. Both develop and continue an individual identity. But don't worry, no one must give up their latkes! However, let me share this quote:

> *It was an old story that was no longer true...Truth can go out of stories, you know. What was true becomes meaningless, even a lie, because the truth has gone into another story. The water of the spring rises in another place. –Ursula K. Le Guin*

The water is rising in the Interspiritual Age. The age of recognizing our interdependence and interconnection with all life, all beings, all others. It is a story of reunion. It is about living with others whom we came to know in the Interfaith Age through the story of recognition. (It may also include intrafaith reunion, a recognition of Jews who have been marginalized by today's dominant Ashkenazi culture. An example of such recognition is the increasing inclusion of Jews of Color. So, now we must ask:

What story can we tell, what song can we sing, what ritual can we perform to embody the meaning of these re-unions?

To reflect this step of Reunion or Integration in the Interspiritual Age, we'll perform a new ritual with our box of Hanukkah candles, for *out of the old comes the new.* Get your candles ready. Refer to the bowl of sand that you prepared in advance. (Hopefully, you read this first.)

This *giant bowl, filled with damp sand* represents Earth. In the center is a *yahrzeit* (memorial) candle, already lit. The light symbolizes the gifts of those who came before us, of those yet to come, and the Source of all gifts, All Existence Itself. At this time, we think of our personal and communal gifts for which we can feel gratitude and a desire to share.

Dim the lights. Consider all the gifts you've received. Take a moment to reflect on your unique gifts. What talents do you bring to the world? Maybe you have a skill to teach us. Or an instrument to play. Maybe you have the solution to a problem. Maybe you know how to download an app and can teach others.

In any order, take turns taking a candle *from the candle dish.* Light your candle from another, for our lights, our gifts, inspire each other. Once lit, place your candle in the *sand,* near the center, and move outward as we progress, spreading our light and making it bigger and brighter (and not burning our hands!). Sharing our gifts, we inspire each other.

As we enact this Interspiritual Age ritual, we'll all sing, *This Little Light of Mine,* until we've each named one of our gifts. But we'll change the words of the song as follows:

"This BIG light of OURS, WE'RE gonna let it shine.

This BIG light of OURS, WE'RE gonna let it shine.

This BIG light of OURS, WE'RE gonna let it shine.

Let it shine, Let it shine, Let Us shine."

This 3-step journey is my gift to you. Plus, a bonus step!

BONUS STEP 4: The Kids' Challenge (Optional)

Many of us play the Dreidel Game during Hanukkah. The rules are designed so that one player wins by accumulating the most coins or coin substitutes. The challenge for players who belong to the World is: *Can you design new rules for the Dreidel Game so that all players have fun behaving cooperatively and interdependently?*

In this game, we all win!

(3)
BEING JEWISH IN AMERICA IN DECEMBER

Although America's dominant religion is Christianity, so far, people of all faiths are welcome. The first of three acts below focuses on being Jewish in America in December, and the second on being Jewish at Christmas. They present joys and challenges of becoming Jewish in the Interspiritual Age.

ACT ONE

The joys and the challenges of interfaith life are amplified in December, the most interfaith time of the year. Every so often, three major holidays in America, Hanukkah, Christmas, and Kwanzaa, overlap. In December 2024, Christmas and Hanukkah met on the same day, a rare event that has only occurred a handful of times (1910, 1921, 1959, 2005). In addition, other holidays like Winter Solstice (Dec 21st), the Swedish holiday of St. Lucia, bearer of light, and in Mexico and the Americas, the Catholic Fiesta of Our Lady of Guadalupe, punctuate the month.

December is so loaded with different religions' holidays that for interfaith families it is called **December Dilemma**. Partners can get tied in knots deciding what holiday to celebrate with which family members, where, and how. In my practice as an Interfaith Coach, I've seen this season cause feelings of **December Disaster**. But it's also an opportunity for reunion after separation and recognition.

I've had my share of December Dilemmas. My responses, as December approached, ranged from freaking out over a tree in the house to insisting our family attend church on Christmas Eve to combat the commercialism of the holiday. There were times I kept the holidays in separate rooms and times I merged them into one, with a Jewish star topping the tree. When it felt competitive, I nixed giving Hanukkah gifts and made us *make* all the Christmas presents. I admit to times when I wanted to do nothing. "Let's *not* celebrate the holidays this year!" (Not recommended if you have children.) Inevitably, *each year,* I sought to cull new and relevant meaning as an interfaith family in a world that resisted recognizing the fullness of multiple belonging.

I turned to philosophy. I wanted the celebration of holidays to reflect a worldview that honors my religion's wise traditions, my husband's, and our local and global neighbors'. I wanted a worldview that values tradition and humanistic values, respects reason and progress, admits where legends end and history begins, and shares its esoteric teachings. I wanted a worldview that celebrates diversity, creativity and truth but doesn't get stuck in "all is good" and "they're all the same" when they're not. Where was a worldview to show, not just say, how we are ALL deeply interconnected? Where was that philosophy of life?

What happened next forever changed my December. I began to step out of my ethno-centric, comfortable worldview. I attended interfaith, inter-religious, and interspiritual conferences. I read books on integral philosophy, underlining whole chapters. I responded to an *evolutionary impulse* to harmonize opposites — creation and evolution, ideas of life and death, and measures of GDP and GNH — not just in my head, but in practice. Then I began designing lessons, ceremonies, and celebrations with an urge to tap into this wider consciousness. Slowly, my worldview expanded.

I had to consider what my worldview is or combination of worldviews and what world was I creating? What is my philosophy of life and my conception of reality? What do I really value? How was my worldview formed and is it open to change?

I then chose to celebrate Hanukkah from a worldview where opposing perspectives are part of a greater whole, a bigger story, with room for the core values of multiple traditions and worldviews. It takes effort to construct this container and courage to live from it. But doing so can turn December's dilemma into December's delight.

ACT TWO

When Hanukkah and Christmas converge, some Jews worry that Hanukkah will be lost in the overlap. One year, *The Times of Israel* asked, *"Is the Jewish community ready for a very merry interfaith Chrismukkah?"*

The article raised the discussion we can imagine taking place in Judea in 165 BCE, leading to the events of Hanukkah. *How much of "not Jewish" — whether Hellenistic culture or American culture — is too much? How much of "what is not Jewish" endangers "what is"?*

The questions are loaded with assumptions about what it means to be Jewish in America (or the diaspora) and what it means to live with or be surrounded by non-Jews. Perhaps these assumptions need to be questioned if Judaism is to be a viable source of meaning and purpose and a resource for wisdom in the world.

With 38 years in an interfaith marriage, much of my life has been dedicated to discerning my relationship to Judaism in that context. I won't go into the story of this ever-evolving struggle (which may define my Jewishness), but I will share what I now do in December.

For years, I joined in my spouse's family tradition of attending a Christmas Eve service at his parent's Presbyterian Church. One year, when Christmas Eve, Hanukkah, and Havdalah (the end of the Sabbath) all happened to coincide, the family's tradition was interrupted by a change in the church schedule. It turned into an opportunity for me to lead a home service for my spouse's entire extended family. The home service I designed celebrated Christmas, Hanukkah, and Havdalah. It was meaningful for everyone.

While my husband's family has roots in Presbyterian and Quaker faiths, extended family members have former affiliations, current leanings, or spiritual interests in a variety of religions including Mormon, Catholic, Buddhist, Hindu, Taoist, Indigenous, and Jewish as well as agnostic, atheist, believer, seeker, spiritual but not religious, and poetic, among other faith styles.

Our home service became a new tradition that has now lasted ten consecutive years. It is one of my greatest joys. My larger family gets to sing their favorite holiday songs and learn new ones, reflect on a theme that speaks to our times, and integrate spiritual teachings and scripture from multiple traditions. (As my mother likes to say, "The Jew in the family leads the Christmas service.") The truth is, I've learned more about the interdependence of our religions than I would without this opportunity.

What makes our home service successful is the openness with which it is received. In this exchange lies the permeability necessary to share perennial wisdom among our world's different and treasured traditions. This is interspiritual.

ACT THREE

How does one follow Acts One or Two if you don't have a big family, let alone a religiously diverse one. This is where we need imagination. We can create opportunities with various religious communities. It takes effort, but it will be worth it. I encourage us to do so.

In Act Three, we fold our ethno-centric system into a larger interspiritual one. We form new coalitions with different faith communities and plan in-person and/or virtual interspiritual experiences and programs. We encourage friendships across faiths so that we can build a foundation for belonging to the World. See the Appendix for ideas.

The next time *The Times of Israel* asks if diasporic Jews are ready for the convergence of Hanukkah and Christmas, I hope I've shined a big light on the answer: Yes! Perhaps the way we reimagine Judaism in the Interspiritual Age will inspire people of different faiths to reimagine theirs as well.

④
PURIM PLUS

Each spring, when **Purim** is celebrated in the Jewish community, I challenge my students — almost all are from interfaith families with at least one Jewish parent — to explore this holiday *alongside* the Hindu holiday of **Holi,** the Sikh holiday of **Hola Mohallah,** the Catholic holiday of **St. Patrick's Day**, and the Persian holiday of **Nowruz**, to name a few. (Note: Some of these holidays were studied after making the poster in the picture.)

I encourage students to learn basic facts about each tradition. Such information is easily found online. *But what cannot be found from a search engine is an understanding and experience of the deep nature shared by these different holy days by meeting people who practice them.*

Since the home religion in our classroom was Judaism, my students learned about Purim in years past. They acted out the story of Queen Esther, the Jewess who risked her life to save her people from wicked Haman's plot to annihilate the Jews. They read the *Megillah* of Esther (the story in scroll form) about this event that took place in the ancient Persian province of Shushan. They dressed up in costumes of the characters, ate *hamantaschen* (cookies shaped like Haman's hat), shook "groggers" (noisemakers to drown out Haman's name in the story), and gave gifts of food to family and friends. Having practiced *traditional* Purim customs, I then led my students into a new field of religious education; I integrated monofaith study with interfaith education and interspiritual experience. You can, too.

Consider asking your students to compare Purim to holidays of different religions that occur around the same time. *What might they learn about these holidays and those who celebrate them? Can they experience these holidays? What might they learn about themselves and others?*

After initial research, your students might see patterns like what mine saw. For example, during Purim, Jews masquerade in costumes based on characters in the story. During Hola Mohallah, Sikhs wear costumes re-enacting mock battles that celebrate their survival and freedom (or *khalsa*). On Saint Patrick's Day, Catholics dress in green. According to a Persian acquaintance, *"Perhaps no other Spring holiday is more closely connected to Purim, [a word from Avestan, the Iranian branch of Indo-European language], than the over 3,000-year-old Persian new year of Nowruz."* Rooted in Zoroastrianism, Nowruz is mostly a secular holiday celebrated by millions of people across ALL faiths in many countries to mark the arrival of spring, renewal, and rebirth.

My students noticed merry making with all of these holidays. Jews are encouraged to drink on Purim (but not too much) as part of the occasion. Similarly, drinking is a familiar hallmark of St. Patrick's Day. They learned that on this feast day honoring the patron saint of Ireland, restrictions of Lent are removed (and hence drinking is allowed). The Hindu holiday of Holi includes squirting red and green colors of paint — colors that manifest divine love— on each other in a playful manner. (Instead of starting in a costume, one ends up in a painted one!)

Things got interesting when my students decided to explore more spring holidays and not only religious ones. My students asked, *"Do all spring holidays include parades with costumes and noise and merry making? What about Mardi-Gras, Chinese New Year, April Fool's Day, the annual college Hash-Bash, and more?"*

In answering for themselves, they realized they could not force all holidays to fit their schema. Did the holidays of Easter and Passover, also occurring in the Spring, reflect the same pattern they were noticing? What about when they learned from their Muslim peers in Jakarta that there is no spring season in that country in which to have a spring holiday. Their analysis relied upon a growing understanding of religion, history, and geography. Their inquiry drew upon developing an interfaith, intercultural, and international awareness.

To deepen inter-religious study, we decided on creating an artful poster to communicate our research and conclusions. Since the interfaith poster of the Golden Rule[109] hangs on our classroom wall, we humorously imitated it, calling ours the *Spring Rules* poster. *(With gratitude to Chava Makman-Levinson for her creative work on the poster!)*

As the class engaged in critical thinking to debate the merits of holidays both religious and secular which reflect a spiritual energy of *release*, a deeper appreciation for our world's diversity evolved. Students saw a connection between religion and cyclical time, tradition and the repetition of nature, psychology and ritual. One student summed it up when he claimed that all these holidays reflect what happens when you go nuts from "cabin fever." These holidays give us permission to reinvent ourselves.

While this exercise is by no means a definitive or final lesson in the teachings these holidays offer, it lays the groundwork for learning more. By learning about other people's religions and cultures, students grow into global citizens with a world-centric perspective to which appreciation of the universe/cosmos can be added. To Belong to the World, in addition to family and tribe(s), THIS we cannot get from isolation in our cabins, or worldviews.

⑤
PASSOVER'S PROCESS

Seder means Order. Passover Seders follow an order of 14 Steps. I won't list them all here, but I will ask you to notice the relationship between Step 4, *Yachatz,* and Step 11, *Tzafun.* Yachatz is about *being broken*, about the splitting of self during slavery, about the Red Sea splitting. It is symbolized during the Seder by breaking *matzah* (the unrisen bread) and hiding the bigger half. Hiding is what we do when we feel shame or fear.

Part of the Interspiritual Age is healing from past traumas. We can help somatically release shame which stays hidden and once protected us in a traumatic event from deeper overwhelming pain.

Tzafun is about *healing the brokenness*, bringing the broken-off part out from hiding into the light. Healing is about coming into wholeness, a new experience. At the Seder, this is symbolized by searching for the broken piece which, once found, is broken into smaller pieces so that all who are at the table may eat of it.

How does *yachatz/broken* become *tzafun/whole*?
Passover is not the only Jewish story of transformation from *yachatz/brokenness* to *tzafun/*wholeness. Let me share two others.

First, during Biblical times, Jews made the pilgrimage to the one and only Holy Temple for major festivals. It was the center of all religious life. When the Temple was destroyed, so was a way of life (*yachatz*). But destruction made space for a new way of life, a new consciousness that was needed to meet the changing times, the changing consciousness. Rabbinic Judaism *(tzafun)* repurposed the previous form of religion. Synagogues replaced the Temple and reintroduced its elements in new ways while rabbis replaced the High Priest and fulfilled those duties in new ways. A new way of expressing Judaism, of becoming rabbinically Jewish, transpired.

Second, the biblical story of God's preference for Abel's sacrifice (sheep) over his brother Cain's (wheat) may not have been as much about offering one's best, or about the attitude with which it was given, as about letting it go. Professor Howard Adelman (z'l), a scholar of Hegel, shared this interpretation.

> *God preferred to recognize the nomadic way of life of the shepherd even as humanity was adopting a sedentary agricultural way of life. The irony is that God's recognition was not for that which was to be valued as historically the superior way of life, but as the way of life that had to be sacrificed to give way to [the new] agricultural societies.*

If Jewish slavery made way for freedom, if the destruction of the Holy Temple made room for Rabbinic Judaism, and if the declining pastoral life allowed for agrarian society, then what is the *yachatz* of today? And what is *tzafun*? For what is our evolution calling us?

You might discuss these questions and your answers during your next Passover Seder with optimism for the new and with patience for the process. After all, there are seven steps between *yachatz* and *tzafun*.

My short answer is that *yachatz/broken* represents postmodern consciousness and its forms of Judaism and other organized religions as we know them. This is not to say that the values of postmodernism aren't necessary. They are critical since we cannot expand consciousness without them. *tzafun/coming into wholeness* expresses a new perspective in the evolution of culture, one that is now emerging.

The new way of doing religion is arriving at its wholeness. Its forms are inspired by interfaith families, interspiritual experience through solidarity within and among different religious groups, and by integral philosophy. Just as it takes time to get from Step 4 *(yachatz)* to Step 11 *(tzafun)* during the Seder, it takes time to spiral from one worldview to the next. In doing so, a worldview capable of solving the problems of the prior age comes into view. Not only will everyone taste a *piece* of Passover, but they might also taste the *peace* of wholeness.

6

TEN PLAGUES OF MONEY

It is not only the way we celebrate and teach religion that gets an update in the Interspiritual Age but how we create new forms in other sectors of society as well. How we value and use money is one of them. In particular, religions have something to say about how to correct the growing inequality of wealth. In Judaism, that correction is called *Shmita* and it is supposed to happen in Israel every seven years followed by a bigger correction every 49 or 50 years, the Jubilee, depending on how you count. *Shmita* means release. It is the name of the seventh year when land and people rest and when all debts are forgiven, according to biblical law.

During the holiday of Passover when Jews celebrate freedom and release from slavery in biblical times, we can use Passover to reconsider our relationship to money. Are we *enslaved* to a certain way of perceiving money? Could changing our worldview result in new forms for the economic sector of our society?

The Seder can be a teaching opportunity to free ourselves and others to form a new relationship with our economy and money. Instead of scarcity as the foundation of the economy (the old worldview), what if the foundation is Abundance? For this reason, I created a *Haggadah* (the program for the Seder) that uses the Jewish story of *freedom from slavery* as a metaphor for *freedom from enslavement to an aging economic perspective* The Ten Plagues of Money (below) offers a glimpse into the Freedom from Money *Haggadah*.

During the Passover Seder, it is a tradition to dip one pinky finger into a glass of wine with the recitation of each plague. Since wine symbolizes joy, we are ritually removing a drop of joy with each dip, to acknowledge that we don't take joy in the plagues, for by nature, they cause harm to us and others, and we should not delight in others' pain. Thus, the plagues below are reminders of what we do NOT want and are meant to inspire a different response to our world.

THE TEN PLAGUES OF MONEY[110]

1. We focus on creating scarcity instead of abundance.
2. We focus on accumulating money instead of circulating it.
3. We focus on believing "more for you is less for me" instead of "more for you is more for me".
4. We ignore the hidden costs of our consumption instead of including them upfront.
5. We focus on owning property instead of owning its improvements.
6. We focus on loaning and borrowing instead of giving and receiving.
7. We focus on monetizing everything (ideas, water, childcare, friendship) instead of sharing.
8. We focus on what we want instead of what someone else needs.
9. We focus on economic growth instead of sustainability and restoration.
10. We focus on fear instead of love.

Throughout the discussion during the Freedom from Money Passover Seder, we begin to see an alternative perspective regarding money, one that includes our market economy and transcends it with a growing gift economy. We hear how money can make some feel crazy and how it can motivate others. By the end of the discussion, we might see the freedom that comes from a new relationship with money based on new values.

Religious festivals can be occasions for stepping back and reflecting on the society we want to be with other members/groups in society. They can encourage us to step into a new worldview and articulate the principles we wish to live by together. But that is not enough. We need to create those tools and institutions and perhaps new money systems that uphold those values. We need to do this with others as co-creators, belonging equally at the proverbial table together. Hopefully, this experience is priceless.

Centerpieces from a 65-person multicultural Freedom from Money Passover Seder.

⑦
INTERSPIRITUAL SHMITA

Taking the ten plagues of money (above) seriously can inspire us to free ourselves from the harm done by our current economic model to experiment with something that supports healing, restoration, and reparations, or coming into wholeness, for all. This essay is about an attempt to do so with my students as they learned about the Jewish holy days of *Shmita* (release) and *Yovel* (Jubilee). Bear with me.

Part of my Sunday School curriculum included a unit on religion and economics. I called it *Religonomics*. In this unit, we compare land, labor, and capital from the perspective of different worldviews. Worldviews hold values that we may adopt without our conscious awareness. Like the allegory of the fish swimming in water who, when asked *How's the water?* wonders, *What's water?* We too are swimming in an environment so obvious that we don't notice it. Part of introducing worldviews and what they value is to make us aware of the water we're swimming in. Otherwise, it's hard to change.

To understand the first lever of economic power, we looked at Land, a part of Nature. In the traditional worldview, Nature is valued as meaningful because it is God's creation. In the modern worldview, with its emphasis on the individual and the value of achievement, hedonism, success, status, and power, Nature becomes an object, a resource for exploitation. Those who own property and control the economy influence the distribution of wealth. In the postmodern or progressive worldview, Nature can be an alternative to church or God and an oppressed entity whom social justice activists rally to protect. Progressives, who call for equality for all people and support post-materialistic values, often have trouble developing power (due to their relativistic view of reality). In the capitalist system, Nature/Land becomes private property, and the ruling government tends to favor property owning rights. Thus, their power maintains a system that harms Nature.

For people of property, says Matt Stewart, the atomic theory of freedom confirms *"their belief that freedom and prosperity is theirs alone... and that the cries for equality are therefore merely a cover for theft."* (The Emancipation of the Mind, p.227) Threatened by equality, people of property tend to see others' freedom as stealing their own. Thus, they try to control who has freedom and who doesn't.

When Rebecca Clarren, prize-winning journalist and author of *The Cost of Free Land,* learned that her Jewish family benefited from lands stolen from the Lakota, she turned to Jewish tradition for insights on how to atone for the injustice. She studied the Talmud and Torah and learned the Jewish system *(teshuvah)* for social justice, repair of harm, restoration of land, and healing relationships. The accountability called for reflects the Interspiritual Age with its emphasis on individual and cultural evolution and growth. As a result, among other efforts, Clarren worked to help Native-led efforts to recover stolen lands in a fair way.

Of course, the first step in any attempt at reparations is to stop the harm and to stop the systems that allow it to continue to happen, so it can't happen again. Clarren's experience as an American Jew with repairing her family's inherited share of the harm done to Indigenous people should be a wakeup call all of us, not only Americans and their relationship with Native American, but Israeli Jews and their relationship with Palestinians. Those complicit in apartheid policies must stop the harm and the systems or structures that allow it and to make reparations. For this reason, it's even more important to become interspiritually Jewish.

Changing how we relate to land, labor, and capital requires more than making amends. It requires a new worldview that allows for forms, systems, and institutions that not only prevent the problem from repeating but supports *"universal values of self-actualization, wisdom, and transcendence."* (de Witt) This emerging worldview integrates the best of prior worldviews while releasing the worst.

According to Annick de Witt, in this emerging integrative worldview (i.e., the Interspiritual Age), Land/Nature is *"spiritually significant, intrinsically valuable, and a partner."* For Indigenous people, this has always been the case. Indeed, the Land and all its plants and animals are their relatives. (For this reason, I capitalize Land and Nature.) We can learn from Indigenous people, especially about relating to Land and Nature, as well as from our Jewish sources. In building trust by learning alongside each other, others can be inspired by our traditions too.

From our home religion of Judaism, my students learned about the ancient Jewish practices of *Shmita* (release) and *Yovel* (Jubilee), biblical injunctions in the Torah; Exodus 23:10 and *Parashat Behar* of Leviticus. These laws, among other things, call for letting the Land lie fallow and the cancellation of all debts every seven years. By not farming for a year, the land gets a break as do the farmers, while canceling debt results in leveling the economic playing field. This led to class discussions about a form of capital, money.

We looked at how money as a medium of exchange changed over time (the gift economy, cowrie shells, commodities, credits and debits, etc.). My older students even joined an extracurricular class on financial literacy and responsibility. We observed the difference between the gift and market economies in terms of how they affect people. We looked at how some countries' debts were forgiven by the International Monetary Fund and explored Jewish and Muslim law regarding charging interest *(ribit/riba)*.

We learned that according to Charles Eisenstein, our monetary system has gotten in the way of our ability to connect to people.

> *Of all the things that deny uniqueness and relatedness, money is foremost...Moreover, as a universal and abstract medium of exchange...a dollar is the same dollar no matter who gave it to you...This sameness deadens the soul and cheapens life.*[111]

Eisenstein argues that we can make our relationship with money more sacred by making it more personal. We wondered if money could be used to create more personal interconnection, a feature of the Interspiritual Age. So, my students and I designed an experiment.

We kicked off our experiment with Frank Capra's film; *Mr. Deeds Goes to Town* (1936). The film touches on themes of wealth distribution and inequality — as relevant then as it is now. Then, each student was given a PARTICULAR $20 bill. Each $20 bill had a note gently attached to it. Here's what the note on the bill said:

Can a $20 bill interconnect us?

Spend this Money meaningfully!

(1) Tell us how you got STUDENT NAME's $20 bill.
(2) Tell us how you spent *this* bill.
(3) Read about how others spent *this* bill.
(4) Tell us how it felt for you to spend *this* bill.

This experiment expires on a particular date.

For its success…

1. FLOW THE MONEY.
If these bills end up at the bottom of a cash register or the back of a wallet, we fail. Keep it circulating!

2. FOLLOW THE MONEY.
Each student sets a story in motion of how a single bill can connect those who use it.

The circulation of each student's twenty dollars now had the potential to tell a story of which any user of that bill could be a part. We directed those who encountered these bills to a website that welcomed them as follows: *If you're reading this because of a particular $20 dollar bill, Mazel Tov! Maybe you did something to earn it. Maybe someone gave it to you. (Happy Birthday!) Maybe you* *found it on the street. Whatever way you got it, did you wonder who had it before? Or who will have it after? What did those people do with it? Was it useful to them? What are you planning to do with this $20?*

I wish I had a great story to tell about one of those bills, but I don't. Was it a failed experiment? No. It made us think about how we can interact around money in more relational ways. Does this have anything to do with religion in the Interspiritual Age? Yes. As we engage in more interfaith education and interspiritual experiences, we will create forms for all sectors of our society that support the values of integral consciousness for our evolution.

⑧
RAMADAN ADJACENT

Celebrating our Jewish holidays from within an interspiritual frame includes how we relate to people of other religions *through* religion. Ramadan, the Muslim holy *month* that commemorates the revelation of the Quran, is like the Jewish holy *day* of Yom Kippur - both involve fasting and fast-breaking with family and community. Here, I want to show how Interspiritual Jews can *connect* to others through others' holidays. Such connection is an integral part of becoming Jewish in the Interspiritual Age.

I know from fasting each year on the Jewish holiday of *Yom Kippur* (Day of Atonement) from sunset to sunset, that it's easier to fast with others who are also fasting. Since Muslim holidays are based on the lunar calendar, Ramadan occurs at a different time each year. We can show support for and appreciation of our Muslim community members by fasting *with* them for one day of Ramadan. Each time I have done so, it has been such a wonderful experience that I now ask, *How can we all join in creating a new tradition of sharing our holidays, like this one?*

Here's one idea for celebrating Ramadan:

First, pick a day to fast with Muslims. When the local Mosque hosted our *Interfaith Round Table*'s monthly meeting during Ramadan, I chose the meeting date which happened to be June 21st, the summer solstice. (Nothing like an extra challenge of fasting on the longest day of the year!)

Second, commit to that day. To make sure I didn't change my mind, I told my Iranian Muslim friend, Nooshin, that I planned to fast. She was thrilled and invited me to her home for *Iftar,* the special sundown meal eaten with others to break the fast. If you don't have a Muslim friend, attend an interfaith program in your community. Most cities have such organizations. Or call the nearest mosque and ask when you can attend an *iftar*.

Third, follow through. Although I missed eating the 4:30 AM pre-fast meal, I learned that not every Muslim eats *suhoor*. It helped that when our Interfaith group met at the mosque, no one brought lunch out of respect for the fasting community. To get a fuller experience, I also chose to pray at the mosque. Having led my students to this same mosque for a Religion Tour (part of my interspiritual classroom project), I was familiar with the space, the separation of men and women during prayers, and the appropriate way to dress. (Don't worry. If you forget a headscarf, someone will loan you one — as they did for me!)

While I had planned to pray alone, our Muslim hostess encouraged me to wait until everyone prayed together, saying it would be more meaningful. She was right. Out of respect, I copied their movements (standing when they stood, sitting when they sat, bowing when they bowed). I prayed silently in my own words. It lasted five minutes.

After prayers, Lamia, our hostess, gave each person in our group (fasting or not) a carry-out container with samples of traditional *iftar* foods. I couldn't help but feel it should have been us providing a meal for them!

That night, when I entered Nooshin's kitchen for my first *iftar*, a feast awaited. The abundance filled me with such love that I felt full and blessed before taking a single bite. We enjoyed walnut-filled dates, exotic yogurt sauce, Nooshin's famous hummus and pita, special French feta, two different aromatic rice dishes, roasted chicken, kofta lamb, salad with fresh mint and sumac, Iranian sweets, and more.

On another occasion, I celebrated an *Iftar* meal with a local Afghan family, the father of whom I had befriended through work. I had been coordinating a private refugee sponsorship circle to help bring his mother and brother to the US and he invited our entire circle including spouses and children to join their meal. It was a special evening and the feast was memorable.

The desire of our group to help reunite members of this Afghan family was met with deep gratitude. Not only did we all enjoy each other's company, but we got to know each other better.

Developing these cross-cultural friendships is critical to the Interspiritual Age.

Through both experiences and others, I learned about Ramadan and its various practices across different Muslim cultures. The image that stands out is of communities laying blankets on sidewalks covered with dish after dish of food for the sundown meal — for all to come and eat, especially those who are hungry and needy. Ramadan cultivates compassion. It made me want to see and experience this compassion in Judaism and to appreciate it when I saw it, for example, at the Passover Seder. This experience of interdependence, of learning about our own and others' holidays through each other, is a feature of the Interspiritual Age.

While Jewish communities do indeed host *Iftar* meals for local Muslims, it's often a one and done event. To really inhabit this worldview, it needs to be part of the foundation, to become part of a tradition. What if Jewish communities committed to building relationships and friendships by sharing in each other's holidays?

This is one way of building solidarity. I urge congregations to form an ongoing relationship with a Muslim community so that supporting each other in different holidays becomes an annual event. Perhaps each year, Jewish families host Muslims at Passover or Yom Kippur, and Muslim families host Jews at Ramadan. The same can be said for forming a shared experience with Christians over a meal during Lent. Similarly, Jewish congregations can accept invitations hosted by other religious communities. This is how we build interdependence and solidarity in the Interspiritual Age.

Interspiritual Judaism places more weight on interdependence - learning about each other's religions to appreciate our own - than on independence from others. In this way, we learn to be *with*, not over others; to *join*, not be separate from others, to *stand with*, not neglect others. We have the power to make each other feel welcome and at home in our distinct traditions. My Muslim friends have certainly made me feel that way. I've done the same for them during the holidays I've hosted. By sharing our holidays, we share our humanity and gain the joy of mutual friendship.

When we *experience, not just read about,* each other's holidays, we learn what they stand for and experience the spiritual traits they cultivate. We develop familiarity and comfort in our world.

St. Augustine of Hippo said, *"The world is a book and those who do not travel read only one page."* Let's Belong to the World and experience it together.

(9)
INTERSPIRITUAL YOM KIPPUR

Interfaith Minister Dave Bell invited me to lead a service about Yom Kippur (Jewish Day of Atonement) at *The Interfaith Center for Spiritual Growth*. Before he became an interfaith minister under the tutelage of Rabbi Joseph H. Gelberman, Dave was a corporate lawyer and building contractor. His passionate story of starting an interfaith congregation, along with Tirzah Firestone's passion to start a Jewish congregation in Boulder, inspired me to start a Jewish-Interfaith congregation in my community. By then, I had accomplished my Adult Bat-Mitzvah, completed my ordination in Rabbi Gelberman's interfaith seminary and my training in his Modern Rabbi program.[112] Thus, I found myself, an ordained minister leading a service about the upcoming holiday of *Yom Kippur* at an interfaith congregation.

In leading an interspiritual day of forgiveness, I first applied the lesson learned from my experience with Bob (Growing with God). I gave people multiple entry points to the service through their own conception of God, from wherever they were in their spiritual path. I asked participants to reflect on their perception of what, for them, is greater than oneself and to consider the nature of this relationship.

Do you have a model or image of God/Goddess/Goodness? Do you have a name for it? What generates your trust in life or this model? Does it change with age? circumstances? health? What about it, if anything remains unchanged? I gave ideas for those who needed something to work with. These included:

1. Theism and Deism (God is Transcendent)
For Theists, God is the Unmoved Mover. Omnipotent. For some, this God watches over us, directs events, and intervenes. This God created the world and then left it to us. God is the Supreme Being, Knows All and is Unchanged by world events.

2. Pantheism (God is Immanent)
God is Nature and Nature is God. God and World are One. There is no difference between God and the World. God is Everything.

3. Panentheism (related to process theology)
God is in the world; the world is in God but they're not the same. The universe is part of God, but God is greater. As the universe changes, God changes, too.

4. Process Theology (God's Transcendent and Immanent)
Philosophical integration of science and theology. God is Becoming. God is the cause of the tendency for self-consciousness to evolve. Change/flux is the basis of reality.

5. Interfaith Theology (God is Universal and Particular)
Draws from all wisdom traditions to enrich and inform one's understanding of the world and our purpose in it. Is more concerned with How to live than What to believe.

Of course, there are many ways to think about or experience "God". *God is Nature, God is Random Change. God is Change with Purpose. God is Evolutionary. God is a Verb. God is Hidden. God is Revealed. There is No God. There is only God. God is Everything. God is Us. God is Nothing. etc.* The point is to create space for all to join in. When we read/hear God, soul, holy, divine, providence, etc., we are to keep in mind *our model*. In case nothing comes to mind, Nothingness *(Ayin)* is also a name of God or No God.

I referenced universal themes of forgiveness from multiple traditions before exploring the similar and distinct approaches to forgiveness in Judaism as practiced on Yom Kippur. With this interspiritual approach, we can:

- bring together people of different faith backgrounds, spiritual paths, or different philosophical worldviews.
- experience variations around a common theme.
- share learning with others through a common experience.
- allow for exploring other traditions; religious, secular or cultural.
- deepen understanding of the purpose behind prayers and rituals.

- promote appreciation of inherited, reclaimed, or self-made traditions.

As Rabbi Zalman Schachter-Shalomi said,

> *As we explore the deep structure of our own traditions, revealing the basic functionality beneath the specific wrappings, we cannot ignore their similarity to those of every other religious and spiritual tradition on the planet. Providence, as well as our own evolutionary perspective, demands that we acknowledge a similar sacred purpose at work in these deep structures, that we learn how others use them for the fulfillment of the Greater Purpose, and how others can aid us in understanding our own use of them.* [113]

When we acknowledge the similarities in the deep structure of our religions, we see universal themes through our particular religions. The universal is in the particular and the particular is in the universal in the same way that in quantum physics, a wave can behave like a particle and a particle like a wave.

> *Quantum Physics is more than physics: it is a new form of mysticism, which suggests the interconnectedness of all things and beings and the connection of our minds with a cosmic mind."*[114]

Quantum physics may be another way of saying "nondual" and it reflects a changing worldview. In this worldview, science and religion can go hand in hand; they need not be at odds. Such harmonization is a feature of integral consciousness according to Steve McIntosh, Ken Wilber, and others. (It is also one of my principles for The Interspiritual Classroom.)

After this introduction, we explored why self-forgiveness follows the requirement for making sincere amends on *Yom Kippur*. Among other rituals, participants learned about the Jewish way of forgiveness and joined in primary prayers. We studied the Jewish concepts of: *teshuvah* (return), *tefillah* (prayer), and *tzedakah* (charity). I introduced similar concepts from the Jain holiday of *Paryushan Parva*, also occurring at that time of year and which I was inspired to share having recently visited a Jain Temple.

Together, Jews, Christians, Muslims, Nones, and more, recited *Ashamnu*, the Jewish prayer for collective forgiveness. We engaged in an exegesis of the Jewish, Christian and Muslim prayers of remembrance: Mourners Kaddish, the Lord's Prayer, and Al Fatiha. We uncovered common themes of adoration, submission, and supplication in these three prayers. Through an interactive, educational, devotional, philosophical, and therapeutic service, we experienced the solidarity of interspiritual practice without forsaking the uniqueness of Judaism or any other religion.

Dave's congregants and visitors to the service, including Jews, reported the following:

"I had a feeling of being part of a whole and not just an individual."
"I will remember the sense of peace and connection I experienced."
"As I read the different models of Go(o)d, I felt a part of all of them."
"What interests me about the way this program combines philosophy, religion and education is just how needed this approach to spirituality is."
"I really liked this program and would definitely participate again."
"I learned a lot more about Yom Kippur than I ever knew and I liked the link to other faiths."
"This program provides a necessary, holistic approach."
"What I experienced was definitely worthwhile!"
"The universality of the need for communal accountability and individual soul searching came through to me in this program."
"I appreciated the religious prayers around a theme, the common threads throughout, and the importance of forgiveness."
"The program captured my interest in science and religion and how the two are coming closer to one another as well as my strong interest in evolutionary theology and spirituality. Thank you for sharing!"

Our religious holidays are richer when we celebrate with others who see the mystical teachings of their religions through ours, and vice versa. Sometimes, when we learn our own traditions through another lens, we deepen our shared humanity. Religious holidays are opportunities to raise the mundane to the sacred and see "God" in each other. If we carry this practice into everyday life, not just on holy days, we cultivate a holy world. We don't have to wait for this. We can be active agents in our co-evolution. Seeing "God" in each other, where others include our treasure trove of great religions, we *become interspiritual.*

⑩
GOOD SHABBOS

The seventh day is a place in time which we build.
It is made of soul, of joy and reticence.
-Abraham Joshua Heschel

In gratitude for reading this far, the final chapter is a gift. It is a takeaway you can use immediately to begin celebrating Judaism in the Interspiritual Age, if you so choose. This essay honors the holiday of Shabbat, the most sacred time of the Jewish week. It includes a guide for how you can celebrate Shabbat in the spirit of the Interspiritual Age. There is no better holiday with which to conclude this section.

First, let me mention the Orthodox Rebbe, Rabbi Menachem Mendel Schneerson, who came to America and led the Chabad movement of Hasidic Judaism. Hasidism focused on reviving the idea of a personal connection with God. I believe interspirituality, awareness of the universal mystical truths at the heart of all religions, is a natural outgrowth of Hasidism, that it is the next stage of our spiritual evolutionary experience of oneness with God (the message of Hasidism) that can lead to the social solidarity called for in these times. Only now, this message transcends the tribe and opens itself to learning from other traditions while also sharing its wisdom.

Rabbi Simon Jacobson, who codified many of the Rebbe's talks, said, "*Although he was a Jewish leader, the Rebbe taught -and embodied- a distinctively universal message, calling upon all humankind to lead productive and virtuous lives, and calling for unity between all people.*"[115]

With this statement, Jacobson captures what I interpret as The Rebbe's embrace and even foresight of the Interspiritual Age. For it is the social solidarity between all people (not only Jews) and the method with which we can affect this unity (productive and virtuous lives) that the Interspiritual Age is realized. The Rebbe's call for unity coincides with the purpose of evolution expressed through the upward, spiral pull towards the Good. *"Each worldview is responding to the pull of the upward current of good in its own way."*[116] The worldview of the Interspiritual Age is responding to that pull.

The interspiritual response to the Sabbath won't look like that of modernism and its ethno-centric worldview, though it will build upon and relish the values it upholds - community, connection, communion, and rest of body and soul. It can, but may not, look like Jews in pews in synagogues praying and yet, the new forms will hold the essence of these former forms. Our new forms will transcend and include former forms to take us closer and deeper to the unity between all people that The Rebbe called for. What then is a new way to celebrate Shabbat that is appropriate for The Interspiritual Age? While there are many answers, I will share one of mine: *A Shabbos Walk.*

My inspiration for the Shabbos Walk came from Ezra Klein's podcast about the Sabbath.[117] Like Klein, I was reminded of what's special about keeping or practicing Shabbat and what I miss and don't miss about it. One thing I missed was the combination of community, leisure, and spontaneity. Going for a leisurely walk with neighbors felt like a good way to get to visit with others (of all religions), to know them and let them know me, to build a local community in our shared physical space, without the fuss of cleaning my house. What's different is that people of all backgrounds are integral to the experience. *During walks, from a place of relaxed oneness, personal spiritual truths can be shared.*

I invited people from all backgrounds who lived within walking distance, to walk together through the neighborhood, to celebrate the end of the work week and the start of a time for rest. Thus began the first chapter of a potential Shabbos Walk Movement.

Here's a guide to leading your own Shabbos Walks for celebrating our different traditions' experiences of rest and renewal, reuniting with others and, for some, with God, in the Interspiritual Age.

JOIN THE MOVEMENT!
BELONG TO A PLACE IN TIME

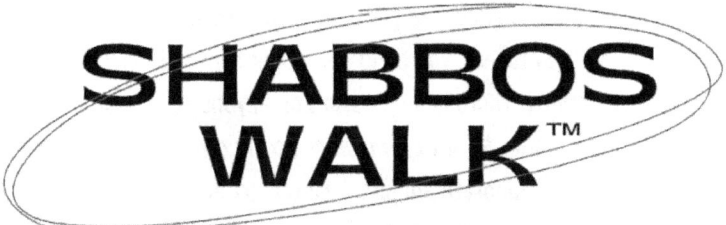

Welcome A TIME OF REST
(what&whenever that means to you)
with a **Joyful Social Walk** in Your 'Hood

What is *Shabbos Walk?*

Shabbos Walk is an opportunity to create a Time for Rest (whatever that means to you, even if you practice it on a different day) by joining in joyful social walks with neighbors in your neighborhood. It should be easy to do with no work involved, no driving to a location for a walk but stepping out your door to walk nearby. It is a Time to know your neighbors and where you live. It is an opportunity to build community among those with whom you share a local place. It is NOT time to proselytize or talk about work or creating, making or unmaking things.

What does *Shabbos* mean?

Shabbos is Yiddish for Sabbath or for Shabbat (Hebrew). It's fun to say *shabbos*. Shabbos means Sabbath which refers to a day or set amount of time for rest and devotion. Rest is different from the activities of work. Shabbos/Sabbath in religious traditions is often devoted to a spiritual practice which can be done alone and/or with others. It is primarily about making time for Nature / God / Spirit / People (family, friends, communities, Others, pets, etc.), for holiness.

Shabbos Walk is not a religious activity, but it can be interspiritual. It is a joyful walk with neighbors.

What is the purpose of *Shabbos Walk?*

Shabbos Walk has several purposes:
1) It is a way for neighbors to get to know each other or know each other better. In the process, you build a stronger sense of local belonging and community. There is no pressure on anyone to host or entertain or clean their home. *No set up, no clean up, no dress up, just show up.*
2) It is a time to celebrate and practice the art of rest.
   No matter what religion, if any, you or your neighbors follow, everyone can agree that social connection during a time of rest is integral to building a shared sense of belonging to a place in time. As Abraham Joshua Heschel said, ***"Labor is a craft, but perfect rest is an art."***
3) It's good for you! Walking is good for everyone who can do it. Walking is also good for people with *shpilkes,* Yiddish for *can't sit still, fidgety, impatient, anxious.* (Wheelchair users and strollers are welcome.)

When does *Shabbos Walk* happen?

This is up to the neighbors! Friday evenings are a time that many people are available to enjoy a leisurely walk after dinner. Friday still signifies the end of the work week and the start of a time for rest even if it's filled with activity. It also happens to be the start of the Jewish sabbath (Friday at sundown) but it doesn't matter. Each chapter can choose the day and time that works best for them.

How do I start a *Shabbos Walk* Chapter?

Easy. Decide to do it one time to get started. Invite a few neighbors. If it goes well, do it again and invite a few more. Eventually, you'll settle on the best day and time for those interested. Take turns organizing and be ready to adapt to a new time.

What about elderly people, babies, kids, and dogs?

Each chapter can decide how they want to handle the needs of different ages in their neighborhood. Some chapters may want two walking groups at different times based on the needs of different age groups. E.g., families with young children may prefer an early morning Shabbos Walk while teens may prefer an evening time. We encourage each chapter to welcome wheelchair users and strollers assuming the neighborhood is safe for wheels. Walking dogs, leashed or unleashed, has a different purpose from Shabbos Walk. We discourage bringing dogs since they pose a tripping hazard. However, each chapter can decide. You do have to pay attention to where you walk. We recommend well paved sidewalks or sides of streets that are empty at times of with no traffic.

Planning Suggestions:
Give your chapter a name. (It can be a neighborhood, an area, a street, or a mascot, etc.) Plan your Shabbos Walks. Plan your preferred method of communication. (Your group may prefer an email with dates in advance or a group text sent on the day of for a spontaneous walk based on the weather.) Keep track of the contact information of those who RSVP for each walk in case you need to cancel.

Ritual Suggestions:
Decide if you want to have an intention or a ritual for your walk. Our chapter meets at one person's house, and we leave there together. We also picked up walkers along the way. We tend to wait several minutes for everyone to arrive at the designated porch. While waiting, we each pick (with eyes closed) an "angel" from a hat or bowl of angel cards. The point is to enjoy the idea that an angel accompanies each of us on our walk dedicated to a time of rest. Often, we share our responses to the angel we randomly. One neighbor who picked Tenderness thought she needed to be more tender with her family members, but another neighbor suggested she needed to be more tender with herself since she had just told a story where she was hard on herself. You can also simply allow each walker to take a moment to set an intention privately for their walk.

Other strategies to make it soulful, joyful, and reticent:
Walk as a group if there is room to do so.
Split up and walk in pairs for more one on one relationship building.
Regularly switch who everyone is paired with. Blow a whistle to indicate when it's time to switch and talk to someone new.
Incorporate time for silence and inward reflection for a certain number of blocks.

Start with a conversation prompt and take turns responding to or discussing it in pairs or all together. Prompts that our chapter has used include: *What does Rest mean to you? What does it mean to say that labor is craft, but rest is an art?*
Read a preselected or random passage from *Sabbath: Its Meaning for Modern Man* by Abraham Joshua Heschel, a leading Jewish theologian, philosopher, and civil rights activist. Add selections on sacred time and rest from other spiritual leaders.

Defining success:
If you strengthen your neighborhood community *in an inclusive way,* that's success. It's even more successful if others also feel a sense of social BELONGING which might be reflected by others showing up and helping plan or organize or add their own touches to the walks in a collaborative way. If there is a sense of social solidarity in your neighborhood, coming together for other events and for mutual aid, that's success. Sometimes, success won't be known until there's a crisis. When a neighbor needs help and can count on those with whom they've bonded through the walks, that's success.

Be Practical:
In bad weather, postpone. Therefore, it's good if walkers RSVP in advance.

Ahad Ha'am, a central literary leader promoting Jewish culture, once quipped, *"More than the Jewish people have kept the Sabbath, the Sabbath has kept the Jewish people".* In the Interspiritual Age, sharing the universal aspects of our traditions keeps us united in our humanity. We all need to rest.

GOOD LUCK AND GOOD SHABBOS!

CONCLUSION

THE INTERSPIRITUAL JEWISH MANIFESTO

Today, there is no longer any question that we need to evolve the way we see, use, practice, celebrate, teach, and relate to and through religions. In T*ablets Shattered*, Joshua Leifer reluctantly offers a prognostication of four possible paths (among others) that American Judaism may go down as it goes down, that is, descends in its long decline. He names the main four as follows: (1) the dying establishment (the mainstream American Jewish institutions of the last century built with posterity in mind), (2) prophetic protest (mainly the young millennial Jewish activists who rediscovered the Jewish cultural call to social justice), (3) neo-reform (today's ritual innovators and liturgical experimenters found in liberal and nondenominational rabbinical schools), and (4) separatist orthodoxy which Leifer describes as today's ultra-Orthodox, "survivors twice over: first of the Nazi mortal threat, then of the liberal capitalist culture on American shores." (p. 323). For Leifer, only the last path is sustainable and promises the survival of Judaism as it has always been known, by *"the commandments that define it and the proscriptions that perpetuate it."* (p. 273)

I understand the concern that Judaism could be lost in alternative and activist Jewish communities. But I've seen Jews rediscover and delight in Jewish culture because of interfaith education. Learning alongside other traditions can inspire us and in turn keep traditions alive.

Leifer's analysis of his four main paths comes through a particular worldview which aligns with the separatist orthodox path he's chosen. This path upholds a traditional value where the self serves social communal norms through conformity, discipline, service, and faith in a theistic, dualistic reality. The other three paths, particularly prophetic protest and neo-reform, represent worldviews with different values. Leifer's choice, despite its shortcomings that even he admits to, is a choice through which he has the freedom to choose because of values upheld by a different worldview, i.e., the modern worldview with its emphasis on individual freedoms.

I believe what is emerging is a new worldview that can hold and value the values of prior worldviews. Hence, these Jewish paths and more may simultaneously include and transcend themselves into a *new way of seeing* Judaism. It is not the various strands of American Judaism that are in decline but the very worldview that has been holding them up. As our dominant traditional and postmodern worldviews converge in a dialectical, seemingly chaotic, nevertheless evolutionary dance, humanity is spiraling into a new worldview and bringing the best of others with it.

If the traditional worldview is about following rules, the modern is about achievement, and postmodern about "what it all means," then the integral or integrative worldview is about making a difference. Values guide decisions and behavior where knowing how to apply which values to which situations for practical solutions matters.

There is evolutionary pressure on humanity to solve its global problems. This pressure is driving a worldview to emerge that allows us to join with our shared values and wisdom resources from all traditions. Teasdale and Teilhard de Chardin were on to something when they said religions must become interspiritual to survive. I hope I inspired us, if not to "reverse engineer" our way to this worldview, then at least to welcome it.

Those who hold an integral or integrative worldview will appreciate the values of all worldviews for their different strengths while avoiding their extremes. To encourage our tribes to move in this direction, I offer the manifesto below. While I don't have all the answers, I hope the *Interspiritual Jewish Manifesto* provides some guidance for going forth.

AN INTERSPIRITUAL JEWISH MANIFESTO

Ten Values

1. Interspiritual Judaism values *integrity* and *connection* - building friendships across religious and cultural and ethnic tribes.
2. Interspiritual Judaism values *intersubjectivity* by which we learn to hold seemingly opposite views at once.
3. Interspiritual Judaism values *interdependence* in studying, teaching, and celebrating our world's spiritual traditions.
4. Interspiritual Judaism values *solidarity* with leaders, teachers, students, and more across faith communities.
5. Interspiritual Judaism values *innovation* to create new forms of religious expression of our spiritual growth while honoring our ancestors.
6. Interspiritual Judaism values *spiritual activism* for social change through 'return' (including reparations and reconciliation).

7. Interspiritual Judaism values *reflective/positive freedom* for expanding our responsibilities in and for the world.

8. Interspiritual Judaism values *evolutionary agency* for manifesting truth, goodness, and beauty in all religions.

9. Interspiritual Judaism values *healing* the wounds of collective trauma for all our tribe and others.

10. Interspiritual Judaism values *harmonizing* ancient mystical wisdom with new discoveries in science.

   Interspiritual Jews belong to the World. They bring Jewish teachings, traditions, interpretations and…their tribe.

ACKNOWLEDGEMENTS

Who knew when I taught Hebrew School as a college student that I would love teaching. I stayed with the same class for over three years. My students came to my wedding, and I kept in touch with them. I still see some of them and their parents. I owe a Big thanks to Aviva Panush for the opportunity to learn that I loved teaching.

Thank you to Barry Checkoway who read my first draft and cheered me on.

Mitch Rycus (z'l) said I had as much right as anyone in the Jewish community to apply for funding when I created *Jewbilation: Jewish Roots with Interfaith Wings* for marginalized interfaith families. Thank you, Mitch (z'l), Carole, and Rita Gelman for giving me the courage and resources to help get it off the ground.

Rabbi Irwin Kula reminded me that, like Abraham, I was paving a new path. Thank you for saying, *"Don't give up,"* in the email I saved from 25 years ago.

Thank you to Rabbi Rami Shapiro for seeing me when I felt invisible and for sharing your perennial wisdom about perennial wisdom.

Thank you to Rabbi Alon Goshen-Gottstein for your gentle wisdom in pursuing a vision that inspires us both.

Thank you to Dave Bell and George Lambrides for being supportive during my early years of interfaith work.

Thank you to Rabbi Nancy Fuchs Kreimer and Dr. Mehnaz Afridi for organizing a life changing interfaith educators conference.

Thank you to my Religion Education Association colleagues and friends, Dr. Sheryl Metzgner, Dr. Elizabeth Nolan, and scholar Paul Hendrik Van Straten, for your guiding presence.

Thank you to all my friends and colleagues in *Face to Face* (Jewish Palestinian Reparations Alliance), *Ann Arbor Circle of Hospitality for Afghan Immigrants (A2CHAI)*, Beth Israel *Zeitouna*, RECIP Academics, and Quiet Spanish. I learn from all of you.

Thanks to many leaders and members of my local Jewish community including Rabbi Elliot Ginzberg, Rabbi Aura Ahuvia, Laurie White, Manya Arond-Thomas, Debbie Field, Michael Appel, Donna Rich Kaplowitz, Ellen Schwartz, Karla Goldman, and Diane Blumson. Your commitment to community inspires me.

Thanks to friends and colleagues who graciously read a version of this book, listened to me talk about it, read early sections, and/or gave suggestions or criticisms that helped me make it better. Even a thoughtfully uttered sentence had the power to influence my writing. Thanks to Jeanine Diller, Julian Levinson, Simone Yehuda, Stan Mendenhall, Diane Falanga, Lucinda Kurtz, Susan Katz Miller, Barry Checkoway, Pastor Joe Summers, Shanti Thirumalai, Janelle Fosler, Elizabeth Walz, Steve Merritt, David Olson, Idelle Hammond-Sass, Margaret Engle, Ernestine Griffin, Vicki Garlock, Ann Gualtierri, Sara Tucker, Anne Dayanandan, Susan Todoroff, Paula Pilarski, Betty Clark, Cathy Antanakis, Nooshin Sobhani, Lorraine Hough, Lenny Bass, Patricia Stepp, Lonnie Ostrander, Julie McCarver, Nancy R. Moritz, Denise Lash, Joan Luby, Galia Peled, Joni Orbach, Rami Efal, Steve Gallinger, Barry Novak, Claudia Kugelmass, Suzanne Keppler, Kelly Willis, and Terri Wilkerson.

Thank you to all the parents and grandparents who participated in *Jewbilation: Jewish Roots with Interfaith Wings* or supported the *Hebrew Play Group (aka Bagels & Blessings)*: Julian, Lisa, Eleanor, Beth, Gaia, Roz, Mark, Rebecca, Megan, Bob (z'l), Elaine, Ben, Megan, Cindy, Deb, Anette, Ed, Nikki, Jon, Gary, Angela, Jake, Cheryl, Lorie, Alan (z'l), and more!

Thanks to my students over the years: Noah R., Amy, Jessica, Alana, Noah G., Sam, Joshua, Gary, Seth, Etta, Stacie, Mara, Rachel, Ian, Jordan, Josh, Aron, Emmett, Zev, Sadie, Saul, Chava, Teo, Jonathan, Mario, Gabe, Elijah, Jonah, Elliot, and more. Each of you taught me to be a better teacher.

Thanks to my mother Eileen, sister Lynn, mother-in-law Ruth and uncle-in-law Jimmy for patient listening and encouragement.

I am grateful to my former professor and friend, Howard Adelman (z'l) who taught me to think critically and inspired me to write authentically.

ACKNOWLEDGEMENTS

Thank you to Clare Kinberg, editor of the *Washtenaw Jewish News*, for believing in me by printing installments of this book.

Thank you to Kate Peterson for all your magical help with anything technical. You are a wizard, in and outside my book.

Thank you to my husband and life partner, Frank Daniel Zinn, for making this journey possible, making me laugh, and loving me every step of the way. I am ever grateful.

APPENDIX: WHAT YOU CAN DO

BELONG TO THE WORLD BRING YOUR TRIBE

In June 2025, Jewish Currents' editor in chief, Arielle Angel, wrote and published an article, *"We Need New Jewish Institutions."* Her article struck a chord. Creating new Jewish institutions is part of creating new forms for Judaism. However, it may not be new physical spaces we need as much as new ideas that become established customs. The Jewish community that sponsored the interfaith Jewish Hanukkah and Hindu Diwali event for both communities two years in a row (see Interspiritual Hanukkah), started such a tradition. Below are more ideas to inspire the expression of Judaism in its new form.

1) Support the formation of *New Interspiritual Communities of Evolutionaries* (N.I.C.E. groups). The Jewish Reconstructionist congregation to which I belong offers weekly zoom gatherings for members to get to know each other. They become a "family" within their community. This idea can be extended to include members of different local religious communities who become a "family" that meets in person and/or zoom. (See your local interfaith round table for help.) These groups can be small interspiritual families, learning from and with each other. Each NICE group can:

- Take turns visiting a museum or commemorative site for each other's communities, together.
- Take turns celebrating a religious holiday *with* each of each other's communities, together.
- Show up for protests, activities, conferences that support their respective causes, together.
- Simply meet regularly to talk about their lives and ongoing faith journeys.

2) Fund the healing of unhealed collective, intergenerational trauma, both with members of your tribe and with an inter-tribal group. Whether we inherited trauma as a victim (and carry shame) or as an oppressor (and carry guilt), meeting with trained trauma therapists/dialogue facilitators can lead to compassionate collective healing. As a matter of public health, this benefits all. Our Jewish institutions could fund these programs making them available to the entire Jewish community. A local, interfaith organization with membership dues from all the different congregations could fund such healing on an inter-tribal -i.e., interfaith, intercultural, interspiritual- level for those who have participated in their tribe's healing work. (Once established, this practice can support the formation of *Alliances for Interspiritual Reparations (AIR), the reconciliation and repair that brings closure to the healing process.*)

3) Fund and promote a Religious Schoolteachers Conference for "Sunday School Teachers" of all religions in your region to learn from each other, build friendships, and plan guest speaking opportunities in each other's classes. Jewish teachers from different Jewish denominations often meet at conferences to improve how they teach Judaism. I want to offer the same kind of program for local (and global) K-12 *religious schoolteachers* so they can share the challenges and successes in teaching their religions. This kind of convening exists for religious academics (AAR, REA) and for public school teachers teaching *about* religion, but we need an Interspiritual forum for "Sunday School" teachers. Imagine what we'd learn from each other and the new programs to emerge.

4) Support interspiritual programs that bring together *leaders and members* of multiple religions. Ideas include:

MEDITATION. Learning about another tradition's meditation practice could inform your own practice, inspire you or others to start a practice, or to go deeper in understanding it. Why not create a program for meditators from each religion to practice together and learn from each other.

ART. The Open Studio Process is a practice that brings people together to make art and kindle creativity in a safe space without judgement. Artist Idelle Hammond-Sass, along with others, applies this process to meaning-making of Jewish texts. Why not offer it to people of different faiths coming together to interpret each other's scripture from their perspectives and thereby discover not only interspiritual truths, but the joy of art.

CHOIR. Singing is a wonderful way to learn about one's tradition. Hymns, chants, *nigguns,* songs, etc. contain spiritual meaning. Why not run a program that brings members of different religion's together to share a song from each one's repertoire. Explore what it means and learn how to sing it. Teach and learn, learn and teach.

DANCE. Dance is another way to connect with one's religious-cultural roots. Why not create a program for people of different faiths to learn each other's dances? Like the other ideas mentioned here, it may increase interest in people learning the dances of their own tradition!

FASHION. When I served on the board of a local Interfaith Round Table, I led a program for the public to meet people of other faiths. It was called *Faces of Faith*. From there, (before Covid and Zoom), we organized in-person *Places of Faith* that allowed people to visit each other's sanctuaries. I wanted a *Fashions of Faith* program as well for participants to learn about each other's different cultural-religious garb. It's not too late to do it.

FOOD. A *Foods of Faith* program can also bring people of different religions together. In 2013, Lynne Meredith Golodner published *The Flavors of Faith: Holy Breads* in which she tells her experience of baking breads from the sacred traditions in Native American, Jewish, Christian and Muslim communities. A cooking class for the members of different religions/cultures in our local community could go a long way towards building social solidarity.

PICKELBALL. It is no secret that many churches with gyms are bringing congregants and non-congregants not into the pew but onto the courts. It is a form of socializing popular with all ages. Why not have a friendly tournament of interfaith teams playing each other.

5) Support cross fertilization of leadership training. Future rabbis, teachers, and communal leaders can be ready to initiate programs between religious communities if they have already formed these relationships. The University of Michigan offers a *Jewish Communal Leadership Program* in its School of Social Work. Why not also support similar programs for future leaders of other religions so these students can begin forming friendships now.

6) Design and implement studies that value interspirituality. Evaluation tools, such as surveys, need to reflect the interspiritual values of integral consciousness so we can track our progress.

Institution-building requires resources of treasure, time, and talent. Mostly, it needs a compelling vision to inspire the funding, education, and training programs described above. An Interspiritual Federation, modeled after Jewish Federation funding, could do the trick. Amen!

NOTES

1. In his poem, *Song of Myself,* Walt Whitman expresses his identity as one with the world. He sensed he was himself and every person he met, that he, and all others, contain multitudes. *Leaves of Grass*: The Complet*e 1891-92 Edition.*
2. The Pew Research Center found that U.S. adults are more likely than people in any other high-income country surveyed to say the Bible *currently* has either a great deal or some influence over the laws of their country. Religious nationalists identify with the historically predominant religion (also often the majority religion) and take a strongly religious position. In the United States, a religious nationalist would be a Christian who says, Being a Christian is very important to being truly American; *And* it is very important that the U.S. president shares their religious beliefs; *And* the Bible should have at least some influence over U.S. laws *And* when the Bible conflicts with the will of the people, the Bible should have more influence. Laura Silver, et al. "Comparing levels of religious nationalism around the world," Pew Research Center. January 28, 2025.
3. In December of 2020, Christians United for Israel (CUFI) issued a press release on its website that it had crossed the 10-million-member threshold. This is larger than the Jewish pro-Israel lobby, AIPAC, with its 3 million members.
4. The Texas State Board of Education is testing the limits of separation by allowing a Bible-based curriculum in the public schools while the Oklahoma state superintendent ordered schools to teach the Bible (though some districts are resisting). Eric Oritz, *Separation of church and state? Religion in public schools is being tested by Christian conservatives,"* NBC News, December 1, 2024. Beth Wallis," *Oklahoma schools resist the order to teach from the Bible in classrooms,"* NPR, September 12, 2024.
5. Clayton Vickers, "*20 percent say violence may be needed to get US back on track: Poll,"* The Hill, April 3, 2024.

6. Mallory Yu, *'Extremely American' explores the Christian theocracy movement in the U.S,"* NPR: All Things Considered, August 31, 2024.
7. Susan Goldstein. *"Rabbi Zalman Schachter-Shalomi Extended Interview,"* PBS: Religion & Ethics Newsweekly, September 30, 2005.
8. Steve McIntosh, *Integral Consciousness and the Future of Evolution*, p. 131.
9. Interfaith America is a Chicago-based non-profit founded in 2002 by Eboo Patel. The organization's stated mission is to inspire, equip, and connect leaders and institutions to unlock the potential of America's religious diversity. Today it operates with roughly 60 full-time staff and a $15 million+ budget.
10. The Council received a grant to run Religious Diversity Journeys. I had the privilege of attending a session where students visited a synagogue. The rabbi taught about Judaism through a mock wedding with the students role playing as bride and groom.
11. Tim Hall, president elect of North Carolina's Social Studies Council, started the website *Religion Matters*, to help teachers improve religious literacy among students in K-12 public schools.
12. The Tanenbaum Center works with institutions, organizations and individuals globally, reaching 4+ million workplace employees, 110,000+ students, and 10,500 medical students and professionals.
13. Emmanuel College of Victoria University in the University of Toronto is one example. The College hosted a conference on interreligious education in January of 2025.
14. A listing of interfaith seminaries can be found here: https://interfaithnet.wordpress.com/interfaith-seminaries-education/ Missing from this list is All Faiths International Seminary https://allfaithsseminary.org/
15. The story serving this purpose may be found in Brian Swimme and Thomas Berry's *The Universe Story*, an autobiography of humanity and the universe as a whole.
16. Steve McIntosh, *Integral Consciousness*, Paragon House, 20p. 124

17. *The White Hotel* by D.M. Thomas, a disturbing novel for its violence, turns Freud upside down. Instead of the past explaining a character's neurosis or PTSD, it is a future event that has not yet happened.
18. From an interview with Krista Tippett, On Being, 2011.
19. I participated with Christian, Jewish, and Muslim educators in a ground-breaking conference for *Emerging and Aspiring Religious Educators* to ask the vital question "What will we teach our children about each other?" The conference was held June 24-27, 2012, at Isabella Freedman Jewish Retreat Center in Connecticut, the result of a partnership between the Retreat Center and the Manhattan College Holocaust, Genocide, and Interfaith Education Center. Conference goals included fostering relationships among future religious educators; exploring existing practices in religious education to contribute to narratives of suspicion, mistrust, and misunderstanding; and exploring potential practices, within communities and through interreligious partnership, that fosters a new narrative promoting respect, understanding, and cooperation.
20. Julia Kristeva, *Strangers to Ourselves* (Columbia University Press, 1994).
21. Alan Morinis, *Everyday Holiness* (Trumpeter, 2008) Chapter 21
22. Steve McIntosh. *Integral Consciousness and the Future of Evolution,* p.84
23. Susan Katz Miller, *Being Both.* (Beacon Press, 2013).
24. Kira M. Newman, "*World Happiness Report Finds That Crises Make Us Kinder,"* Greater Good Magazine, March 21, 2023
25. Dr. John F. Haught, Ph.D., a Senior Fellow of the Woodstock Theological Center and Distinguished Research Professor in the Department of Theology at Georgetown University. He taught religion and science for 35 years at Georgetown. He wrote *God and the New Atheism: A Critical Response to Dawkins, Harris and Hitchens* (Westminster John Knox Press)
26. Carter Phipps, *Evolutionaires* (Harper Perennial, *2012*).
27. Jay Michaelson. Ibid, p.4.
28. The title of this essay alludes to the Buddhist saying, "If you meet the Buddha on the road, kill him" meaning to remove the idolization of ideas that inhibit growth. Another way to

say this is to be careful not to mistake the finger pointing at the moon with the moon.
29. The underlying assumption is that children can handle only one religion. But this has been challenged by "Being Both" communities where children grow up celebrating the religions of both parents in an interfaith family. See Susan Katz Miller, *Being Both*. (Beacon, 2013)
30. Martha Martin, *"Stephen Prothero, scholar, says Americans are religiously illiterate,"* Broadview Magazine, February 1, 2014.
31. See my next book, *The Interspiritual Classroom*, as a resource.
32. Judith Burns. "Religious education in England 'needs an overhaul'," *BBC News*, Nov 27, 2015.
33. "...while philosophy may be of little use in the achievement of the higher levels of personal spiritual progress, it can be very useful in building a functional, pluralistic spiritual community." McIntosh, *Integral Consciousness*, 131.
34. Carter Phipps refers to Hegel's declaration that "the Truth is not only the result of philosophy...the truth is the whole in the process of development...Any cultural or philosophical truth only becomes clear when seen in the light of a larger framework of development." Phipps, *Evolutionaries*, 189.
35. Matthew Lipman, Institute for the Advancement of Philosophy for Children, https://www.montclair.edu/iapc/
36. I have summarized Garry Davis' life from an excellent obituary by Margalit Fox. *"Garry Davis, Man of No Nation Who Saw One World of No War, Dies at 91,"* in The New York Times, July 28, 2013.
37. Ibid., Not to be confused with "The Man Without a Country" a short story by American writer Edward Everett Hale, first published in *The Atlantic* in Dec 1863.
38. Parag Khanna, *Connectography: Mapping the Future of Global Civilization*.
39. "...higher global citizen identification was associated with greater endorsement of both "helping others" ...and "doing something good for society." *"A world together: Global citizen identification as a basis for prosociality in the face of COVID-19,"* Sage Journals. 2023 Vol 26, Issue 1. https://doi.org/10.1177/136843022110516
40. I could not resist a play on words with the song, *A New-Fangled Preacher Man*, from the musical, Purlie.

41. Interfaith Dialogue is used interchangeably with Interreligious Dialogue, but tends to emphasize the sharing of the specific faith dimensions, inner motivations, spiritual practices, ritual expressions, and personal religious experiences across traditions. It also highlights the search for a common basis of spiritual experience and faith among all people. Beverly Lanzetta at beverlylanzetta.net
42. Gurdwara (Punjabi: ਗੁਰਦੁਆਰਾ, Gurduārā or ਗੁਰਦਵਾਰਾ, Gurdwārā; meaning "door to the Guru" is a place of worship for Sikhs; however, people from all faiths, and those who do not profess any faith, are welcomed in the Sikh Gurdwara.
43. Langar (Punjabi: ਲੰਗਰ, Hindi: लंगर) is the term used in the Sikh religion for the common kitchen/canteen where food is served in a Gurdwara to all the visitors (without distinction of background) for free.
44. In Hindu philosophy, prakriti is our elemental nature and vikriti is the imbalance that results when we are not living in harmony with that nature.
45. In Jewish religious thought, every human being has two inclinations or instincts, one pulling upwards, the other downwards. These are the 'good inclination'—yetzer ha-tov—and the 'evil inclination'—yetzer ha-ra.
46. Prasad (Hindustani pronunciation: [prəsaːd̪]; also called prasada or prasadam) is a material substance of food that is a religious offering in both Hinduism and Sikhism. It is normally consumed by worshippers.
47. The Jewish mystical doctrine known as "Kabbalah" ("Tradition") is distinguished by its theory of ten creative forces that intervene between the infinite, unknowable God ("Ein Sof") and our created world.
48. Interspiritual is a term coined by Wayne Teasdale to express the assimilation of insights, values, and spiritual paths from the various religions and their application to one's own inner life and development. Further, the prefix inter in "interspirituality" expresses the ontological roots that tie the various traditions together and the essential interdependence of the religions. (Beverly Lanzetta at beverlylanzetta.net)
49. Matthew Stewart, *An Emancipation of The Mind*, p. 227.
50. Ibid., p. 228

51. Ibid., p. 240
52. Nicole Weisensee Egan. *Fathers Who Lost Daughters in Amish Schoolhouse Massacre Reveal They Are Still Healing 10 Years Later,* People. October 2, 2016.
53. "Gabor Mate: It's like Watching Auschwitz on TikTok," Middle East Monitor. October 17, 2024.
54. *"Nearly four in ten Christian nationalism Adherents (38%) and three in ten Sympathizers (30%) agree that "because things have gotten so far off track, true American patriots may have to resort to violence to save the country," compared with only 15% of Skeptics and 7% of Rejecters."* PRRI analysis of Christian Nationalism. February 4, 2025. https://www.prri.org/research/support-for-christian-nationalism-in-all-50-states/
55. In November 2023, I had the pleasure of speaking with Michael Barnett, renowned international relations consultant, professor at GW, and co-author of "Israel's One-State Reality" in *Foreign Affairs* April 2023. Judaism, he said, needs to detangle itself from Israel.
56. *Israelism* is a 2023 documentary film by two young American Jews raised to unconditionally love Israel. The term refers to the idea that Jews of recent generations were raised with Israelism, not Judaism. When the filmmakers witness the brutal way Israel treats Palestinians, they join a movement of young American Jews seeking to redefine Judaism's relationship with Israel. https://www.israelismfilm.com/
57. Alan Cooperman and Gregory Smith, *A Portrait of Jewish Americans,* Pew Research Center, October 1, 2013.
58. Gregory A. Smith and Alan Cooperman, *"Has the rise of religious Nones come to an end in the US?"* Pew Research Center, January 24, 2024
59. Susan Katz Miller, *"Interfaith Families and Identities in Pew's New Religious Landscape Study,"* Being Both Website, February 28, 2025. https://onbeingboth.wordpress.com/
60. Katz Miller, *Being Both.*
61. Scott Detrow, *"As Israelis protest authoritarianism, Palestinians say their fight remains ignored,"* National Public Radio, April 2, 2023.

62. Marc Tracy, 'No Other Land', Whose Politics Deterred Distributors Wins Best Documentary, *The New York Times*, March 2, 2025.
63. Ibid., "A Portrait of Jewish Americans," Pew Research Center, October 1, 2013. https://www.pewresearch.org/religion/2013/10/01/jewish-american-beliefs-attitudes-culture-survey/
64. *Jewish Voices for Peace* and *If Not Now,* deserve extra credit not because of anti-Zionism but because of anti-Anti-Palestinianism.
65. Eboo Patel, *Sacred Ground* (Beacon Press, 2013) pp.15-17
66. I had been introduced to Sam Bahour via email a decade earlier. We tried to create a pen pal email exchange between our young daughters, but it failed because he never had reliable internet in the West Bank due to Israel's control and abuse of the electrical power.
67. Daniel Gordis, "Modern Israel is our very Last Chance," *Israel from the Inside,* March 22, 2023. https://danielgordis.substack.com/p/modern-israel-is-our-very-last-chance
68. Thomas Friedman, *American Jews, You Have to Choose Sides*, The New York Times, March 7, 2023. https://www.nytimes.com/2023/03/07/opinion/benjamin-netanyahu-israel-protests.html
69. Sammy Smooha, "Israel as a Non-Liberal Democracy," Holy Blossom Tempe's Israel Dialogues, Toronto, February 23, 2023. https://www.youtube.com/watch?v=WRhNicea-YY
70. Razi Nabluse, *Why the main players behind the Israeli protest movement are bringing the confrontation to a head*, Mondoweiss, March 27, 2023
71. Nathaniel Berman, "Israel's Supreme Court is No Human Rights Savior, *HaAretz,* February 14, 2023. https://www.haaretz.com/israel-news/2023-02-14/ty-article-opinion/.premium/israels-supreme-court-is-no-human-rights-savior-just-ask-the-palestinians/00000186-4f2d-d603-a7bf-cfbfe0360000
72. Rania Hammad and Jonathan Ofir, *The Blue and White-Washing Behind Israeli Calls for Democracy,* Mondoweiss, March 10, 2023.

https://mondoweiss.net/2023/03/the-blue-and-white-washing-behind-israeli-calls-for-democracy/

73. Charles Krauthammer was an American political columnist and pundit. In 1987, he won the Pulitzer Prize for his columns in *The Washington Post*.
74. This was said by a Palestinian as quoted by Rabbi David Cooper, *Why I Helped Build a Freedom Camp in the West Bank*, The Jewish News of Northern California, June 7, 2017.
75. Rabbi Michael Strassfeld, *Judaism Disrupted*. Ben Yehuda, 2023.
76. Liberal democracy emphasizes the separation of powers, an independent judiciary, and a system of checks and balances between branches of government. But this form of government, like illiberalism, is nation centric. In the Interspiritual Age, governments will adapt into forms that fit world-centric thinking.
77. Rabbi Burt Jacobson, "Israel, Palestine, and the Ba'al Shem Tov." *Kehilla Community Synagogue,* May 24, 2024. https://kehillasynagogue.org/israel-palestine-and-the-baal-shem
78. To learn more about Face-To-Face, please visit https://kehillasynagogue.org/face-to-face/
79. Ibid.
80. Peter Beinart, "Divided Against Myself in Israel," *Substack: The Beinart Notebook,* July 17, 2023
81. Peter Beinart, "Loving Jews Whose Views We Hate," *Substack: The Beinart Notebook,* July 24, 2023
82. Peter Beinart, "Teshuvah: A Jewish Case for Palestinian Refugee Return, *Jewish Currents,* May 11, 2021.
83. An allusion to the story of a man who proclaims that he will convert to Judaism if the great rabbis can teach the whole of Torah while standing on one foot. Rabbi Shamai sends the man away. But Rabbi Hillel says, "What is hateful to you, do not do to your neighbor. The rest is commentary."
84. Shane Burley, "A Reconstructionist Reckoning," *Jewish Currents,* January 30, 2025.
85. "33% of adults under 30 say their sympathies lie either entirely or mostly with the Palestinian people, while 14% say their sympathies lie with the Israeli people." Laura Silver, "Younger Americans Stand Out in their views of the war," *Pew Research Center,* April 2, 2024

86. I am encouraged by *A New Way (Efshar Acheret)*, an Israeli nonprofit that brings Jewish and Arab high school students together to study for a shared matriculation exam. Jewish and Arab students do not go to the same schools or study together. After attending the first multicultural meeting, one Jewish student said, "It was a unique experience to visit an Arab school and feel comfortable and unafraid." Such efforts need to be multiplied for students of all ages everywhere, not just Israel/Palestine.. *Washtenaw Jewish News*, February 2025, p. 5
87. The number of Jews who study/teach Buddhism is disproportionately large compared to people of other religions and this relationship goes back to the late 19th century if not further. Rich Tenorio, "Studying US Buddhist centers, researcher finds 130-year history of fellow Jews." *The Times of Israel,* April 5, 2020.
88. R. Tirzah Firestone, *Wounds Into Wisdom*, Adam Kadmon, 2019.
89. Kathryn Post, *"After a decade of controversy, clergy psychedelic study is published,"* Religion News Service, June 2, 2025.
90. Ben Harris, *"Meet Rick Doblin, the Jewish psychedelics advocate working to turn a club drug into legal medicine,"* JTA, Nov 19, 2020.
91. In 2013, I had the pleasure of meeting *World Encounters f*ounder, Brian Carwana, at NAIN Connect. His program is a crash course in world religions complete with visits to worship sites and meetings with practitioners. It's popular with teachers in the summertime.
92. Hebrew Language Academy with a website https://hebrewpublic.org/schools/hla/
93. On February 23, 2014, I attended an unprecedented event on Jewish education where nationally recognized Jewish leaders and Hebrew language educators convened to discuss optimal forms of Jewish education in America. The emphasis was on immersion in a non-immersive society. The tone was frightening to me, and the attitude of the panel to interfaith was both hostile and dismissive.
94. Ben Sales, *"Michael Chabon attacks Jewish in-marriage and Israel's occupation in speech to rabbinical students,"* Jewish Telegraphic Agency, May 25, 2018.

95. Albert O. Hirschman, *Exit, Voice, and Loyalty: Responses to Decline in Firms, Organizations, and States,* Harvard University Press, 1970.
96. Muslims in Kolkata, India have been caring for three synagogues ever since the Jews left and they hope Jews will return to fill them. Nina Strochlic, "Meet the Muslim Family who looks after a Jewish Synagogue in India," *National Geographic,* February 26, 2019. This story is inspiring for how we can mutually care for our religions.
97. Roger Kamentz, *The Jew in the Lotus,* (Harper One, 2007)
98. Steve McIntosh, *The Presence of the Infinite,* Quest Books, 2015. 172-3.
99. Michael Lipka, "*U.S. Jews know a lot about religion – but other Americans know little about Judaism,*" Pew Research Center, August 1, 2019.
100. Rabbi Jonathan Sacks, *From Optimism to Hope,* pp. 21-22.
101. *Counting Inconsistencies: An Analysis of American Jewish Population Studies, with a Focus on Jews of Color,* Counting Inconsistencies - 05202019a - CDN
102. Rabbi Rami Shapiro, *Judaism Without Tribalism,* (Monkfish, 2022)
103. McIntosh, *Integral Consciousness,* p. 130
104. Thomas Kuhn, *The Structure of Scientific Revolutions* (University of Chicago Press, 2012) First published 1962.
105. McIntosh, *Integral Consciousness,* p. 34
106. Robert Siegel with Simon Schama. "Hanukkah's Real (and Imagined) History," *National Public Radio,* Dec 12, 2014.
107. Hillel vs History at Chanukah https://www.patheos.com/resources/additional-resources/2011/12/hillel-history-at-chanukah-anna-batler-12-21-2011.
108. David Sasha, *Notes on Hanukkah...* Dec 1, 2010, Mondoweiss, https://mondoweiss.net/2010/12/notes-on-hanukkah-the-maccabees-and-zionisms-invented-traditions/
109. The Golden Rule poster was designed by Paul McKenna. https://www.scarboromissions.ca/golden-rule/the-golden-rule-poster-a-history
110. *Freedom from Money: An Interspiritual Haggadah by Lauren Zinn.*
The inspiration for these plagues came from *Sacred Economics* by Charles Eisenstein.

111. Eisenstein, *Sacred Economics*, p. 8
112. I was also inspired by Rabbi Tirzah Firestone's story in *With Roots in Heaven*. Dave's passion to found an interfaith congregation and Tirzah's passion to start a Jewish congregation (in Colorado) gave me the courage to start *Jewbilation: Jewish Roots with Interfaith Wings*, a Jewish-Interfaith congregation, which I led for six years.
113. Rabbi Zalman Schachter-Shalomi, *Foundations of the Fourth Turning of Hasidism: A Manifesto*, his final book co-authored by Netanel Miles-Yépez.
114. Quantum theory is strikingly similar to nondual philosophy and the noosphere. Google Search. 2025.
115. Rabbi Simon Jacobson, *Toward a Meaningful Life: The Wisdom of the Rebbe Menachem Mendel Schneerson*, p.xv.
116. Steve McIntosh, Developmental Politics. Page 155
117. Ezra Klein, "Sabbath and the Art of Rest," The Ezra Klein Show, New York Times. January 23, 2023.
118. Richa Karmarkar, *"He brought 19 guests to the Maha Kumbh. They share their spiritual experience in a new book."* Religion News Service, November 28, 2025.

BIBLIOGRAPHY

Adelman, Jeremy. *Worldly Philosopher: The Odyssey of Albert O. Hirschman.* Princeton University Press, 2013.

Barnett, Michael, Nathan Brown, Marc Lynch, & Shibley Telhami. "Israel's One -State Reality." *Foreign Affairs, May/June 2023.* Published April 14, 2023.

Beinart, Peter. *Being Jewish After the Destruction of Gaza,* Knopf, 2025.

Beinart, Peter. "Teshuvah: A Jewish Case for Palestinian Refugee Return, *Jewish Currents,* May 11, 2021.

Beinart, Peter. "Divided Against Myself in Israel." *Substack: The Beinart Notebook,* July 17, 2023.

Beinart, Peter. "Loving Jews Whose Views We Hate." *Substack: The Beinart Notebook,* July 24, 2023.

Berman, Nathaniel. "Israel's Supreme Court is No Human Rights Savior," *HaAretz,* February 14, 2023.

Burley, Shane and Ben Lorber. *Safety Through Solidarity: A Radical Guide to Fighting Antisemitism.* Melville House, 2024.

Burley, Shane. "A Reconstructionist Reckoning." *Jewish Currents,* January 30, 2025.

Burns, Judith. "Religious Education in 'Needs an Overhaul'," *BBC.* November 27, 2015.

Clarren, Rebecca. *The Cost of Free Land: Jews, Lakota, and an American Inheritance.* Viking, October 3, 2023.

Cohen, Stanley. *States of Denial: Knowing about Atrocities and Suffering.* Polity Press, March 5, 2001.

Cooper, Rabbi David. "Why I Helped Build a Freedom Camp in the West Bank," *The Jewish News of Northern California.* June 7, 2017.

Cooperman, Alan and Gregory Smith. "A Portrait of Jewish Americans*," Pew Research Center,* October 1, 2013

Detrow, Scott. "As Israelis protest authoritarianism, Palestinians say their fight remains ignored," *All Things Considered: National Public Radio*, April 2, 2023.

Egan, Nicole Weisensee. *"Fathers Who Lost Daughters in Amish Schoolhouse Massacre Reveal They Are Still Healing 10 Years Later," People*, October 2, 2016.

Eisenstein, Charles. *Sacred Economics: Money, Gift & Society in the Age of Transition*. North Atlantic Books, 2011 (Revised edition 2021)

Epstein, Daniel. *Portraits in Faith*. Interview with Tirzah Firestone. November 2018. https://portraitsinfaith.org/reb-tirzah-firestone/

Erikson, Erik H. *Childhood and Society* 2nd ed. Edition. W. W. Norton & Company, 1993.

Firestone, Rabbi Tirzah. *Wounds Into Wisdom: Healing Intergenerational Jewish Trauma*. Adam Kadmon, 2019.

Firestone, Rabbi Tirzah. *With Roots in Heaven: One Woman's Passionate Journey into the Heart of Her Faith*. Dutton Adult, 1998.

Ford, Peter. "Less Nationalism? In Poll, Majority See Themselves as 'Global Citizens'," *Christian Science Monitor,* April 29, 2016.

Fox, Margalit. " Garry Davis Man of No Nation Dies at 91," *New York Times*, July 28, 2013.

Friedman, Thomas L. "American Jews, You Have to Choose Sides," *The New York Times*, March 7, 2023 (accessed March 2025)

Goldstein, Susan. "Rabbi Zalman Schachter-Shalomi Extended Interview," *PBS: Religion & Ethics Newsweekly*, September 30, 2005.

Gordis, Daniel "Modern Israel is our very Last Chance," *Israel from the Inside with Daniel Gordis*. Substack, March 22, 2023. (Accessed March 2025)

Gottlieb, Rabbi Lynn. *Shomeret Shalom: Replanting Seeds of Jewish Revolutionary Nonviolence after October 7*. A chapbook from Pushcart Judaica, 2024.

Greenberg, Rabbi Yitz. *The Triumph of Life: A Narrative Theology of Judaism*. The Jewish Publication Society, 2024.

Gregory, Maughan Rollins and Olivier Michaud, "Philosophy for Children as a Form of Spiritual Education," Montclair State University Digital Commons, December 2022. 10.12957/childphilo.2022.69865

Hammad, Rania and Jonathan Ofir. "The Blue and White-Washing Behind Israeli Calls for Democracy," *Mondoweiss,* March 10, 2023.

Hari, Johann. *Lost Connections: Uncovering the Real Causes of Depression and the Unexpected Solutions.* Bloomsbury, January 23, 2018.

Haught, John F. *God After Darwin: A Theology of Evolution.* Routledge, 2007.

Hegel, G.W.F. *Phenomenology of Spirit.* Revised ed. Edition A. V. Miller (Translator). Oxford University Press, 1977.

Heschel, Abraham Joshua. *The Sabbath: Its Meaning for Modern Man by Abraham Joshua Heschel.* Farrar, Straus and Girouz, 1951.

Jacobson, Rabbi Burt. "Israel, Palestine, and the Ba'al Shem Tov." *Kehilla Community Synagogue,* May 24, 2024. https://kehillasynagogue.org/israel-palestine-and-the-baal-shem-tov/

Jacobson, Rabbi Simon. *Toward a Meaningful Life: The Wisdom of the Rebbe Menachem Mendel Schneerson.* William Morrow, 2017. (originally published 2004)

Johnson, Doug. *Religion, The Missing Dimension of Statecraft.* Oxford University Press, 1994.

Johnson, Kurt, and David Robert Orrd. *The Coming Interspiritual Age.* Namaste Publishing, 2013.

Kamenetz, Rodger. *The Jew in the Lotus.* Harper One, 2007.

Khanna, Parag. *Connectography: Mapping the Future of Global Civilization.* Random House, 2016.

Khatib, Suleiman and Penina Eilberg-Schwartz. *In This Place Together: A Palestinian's Journey to Collective Liberation.* Beacon Press: April 19, 2022.

Klein, Ezra. "Sabbath and the Art of Rest." The Ezra Klein Show. Apple Podcasts. January 3, 2023.

Kristeva, Julia. *Strangers to Ourselves*. Columbia University Press, 1994.

Kuhn, Thomas. *The Structure of Scientific Revolutions*. University of Chicago Press, 2012. (First Press, 1962)

Kuttab, Jonathan. *Beyond the Two-State Solution*. Non-Violence International: January 14, 2021

Lappe, Rabbi Benay. "Episode 200 - Educating Ourselves," *Judaism Unbound*. December 13, 2019.

Leifer, Joshua. *Tablets Shattered: The End of An American Jewish Century and the Future of Jewish Life*. Dutton, 2024.

Lifton, Robert J. & Erik Olson. *Explorations in Psychohistory: The Wellfleet Papers*. Simon and Schuster, 1975.

Lipka, Michael. "U.S. Jews know a lot about religion – but other Americans know little about Judaism," *Pew Research Center*, August 1, 2019.

Magid, Shaul. *The Necessity of Exile: Essays from a Distance*. Ayin Press, 2023.

Martin, Martha. "Stephen Prothero, Scholar, Says Americans are Religiously Illiterate." *Broadview,* February 1, 2014.

McIntosh, Steve. Developmental Politics: How American Can Grow Into a Better Version of Itself. Paragon House, 2020.

McIntosh, Steve. *Integral Consciousness and the Future of Evolution*. Paragon House, 2007.

McIntosh, Steve. *The Presence of the Infinite: The Spiritual Experience of Beauty, Truth, and Goodness*. Quest Books, 2015.

Michaelson Jay. *God is Everything: The Radical Path of Nondual Judaism*. Trumpeter, 2009.

Miller, Susan Katz. *Being Both: Embracing Two Religions in One Interfaith Family*. Beacon Press, 2013.

Morinis, Alan. *Everyday Holiness: The Jewish Spiritual Path of Mussar.* Trumpeter, 2008.

Nabluse, Razi. "Why the main players behind the Israeli protest movement are bringing the confrontation to a head." *Mondoweiss,* March 27, 2023.

Newman, Kira M. "World Happiness Report Finds That Crises Make Us Kinder," *Greater Good Magazine,* March 21, 2023.

Oritz Eric. "Separation of church and state? Religion in public schools is being tested by Christian conservatives," *NBC News,* December 1, 2024.

Palmer, Parker. *Let Your Life Speak: Listening for the Voice of Vocation,* Jossey- Bass, 2024 (First pub 1999).

Patel, Eboo. *Sacred Ground: Pluralism, Prejudice, and the Promise of America.* Beacon Press, 2013.

Phipps, Carter. *Evolutionaries: Unlocking the Spiritual and Cultural Potential of Science's Greatest Idea.* Harper Perennial, 2012.

Piketty, Thomas. *Capital in the 21st Century.* Belknap Press, August 14, 2017.

Prothero, Stephen. *God Is Not One: The Eight Rival Religions That Run the World - and Why Their Differences Matter.* HarperOne, 2010.

Prothero, Stephen. *Religious Literacy: What Every American Needs to Know--And Doesn't.* HarperOne, 2007.

PRR Staff, "*Support for Christian Nationalism in All 50 States: Findings from PRRI's 2024 American Values Atlas,*" February 4, 2025

Sacks, Rabbi Jonathan. *From Optimism to Hope.* Bloomsbury Continuum: July 18, 2004.

Sage Journals. "A world together: Global citizen identification as a basis for prosociality in the face of COVID-19," Vol 26, Issue 1. 2023.

Sasha, David. "Notes on Hanukkah: The Maccabees and Zionism's Invented Traditions," *Mondoweiss,* December 1, 2010

Shapiro, Rabbi Rami. *Judaism Without Tribalism: A Guide to Being A Blessing to All the Peoples of the Earth.* Monkfish Book Publishing, 2022.

Siegel, Robert with Simon Schama. "Hanukkah's Real and Imagined History," *All Things Considered, National Public Radio,* Dec 12, 2014.

Silver, Laura, Jonathan Evans, Maria Smerkovich, Sneha Gubbala, Manolo Corichi and William Miner. "Comparing Levels of Religious Nationalism Around the World." *Pew Research Center,* January 28, 2025.

Silver, Laura. "Younger Americans stand out in their views of the Israel-Hamas war," *Pew Research Center,* April 2, 2024.

Smith, Christian. *Why Religion Went Obsolete: The Demise of Traditional Faith in America.* Oxford University Press, 2025.

Smith, Gregory A. and Alan Cooperman, "Has the rise of religious Nones come to an end in the US?" *Pew Research Center*, January 24, 2024.

Smooha, Sammy." Israel as a Non-Liberal Democracy," Holy Blossom Temple: The Israel Dialogues, Toronto. (February 2023)

Snyder, Tim. *On Freedom.* Crown, September 17, 2024.

Somerson, Wendy Elisheva. *An Anti-Zionist Path to Embodied Jewish Healing: Somatic Practices to Heal Historical Wounds, Unlearn Oppression, and Create a Liberated World to Come.* North Atlantic Books, Berkeley, CA, 2025.

Soules, K. E., & del Nido, D. (2025). Mapping the Field of K-12 Religious Literacy Education: A Working Report. *Religion & Education, 52*(1–2), 32–57.

Spira, Rupert, "The Essence of Meditation Series: Being Myself," *Sahaja Publications*, 2021.

Stewart, Matthew. *An Emancipation of The Mind: Radical Philosophy, the War over Slavery, and the Refounding of America.* Norton, 2024

Staff for A New Way. "Building Bridges in Central Galilee for a Shared Future," *Washtenaw Jewish News,* February 2025.

Strassfeld, Rabbi Michael. *Judaism Disrupted: A Spiritual Manifesto for the 21st Century.* Ben Yehuda Press, 2023.

Strochlic, Nina. "Meet the Muslim Family who looks after a Jewish Synagogue in India." *National Geographic*, February 26, 2019. (accessed March 2025)

Swimme, Brian, and Thomas Berry. *The Universe Story: From the Primordial Flaring Forth to the Ecozoic Era--A Celebration of the Unfolding of the Cosmos.* Harper One, March 11, 1994.

Sucharov, Mira. *Identity, Social Justice, and Learning Communities in the Age of Contested Campus Politics,* University of the Pacific Law Review, Volume 54, Issue 4, July 2023.

Tarnas, Richard. *Cosmo and Psyche: Intimations of a New World View.* Plume, April 24, 2007.

Teasdale, Br. Wayne. *The Mystic Heart: Discovering a Universal Spirituality in the World's Religions.* New World Library, 2001.

Teilhard de Chardin, Fr. Pierre. *The Phenomenon of Man.* Harper & Brothers, 1959.

Thomas, D.M. *The White Hotel.* Penguin Publishing, September 1, 1993.

Tracy, Marc. "'No Other Land,' Whose Politics Deterred Distributors, Wins Best Documentary," *The New York Times,* March 2, 2025.

van der Braak, André. The Study of Mystical Experiences and Latour's Ontological Turn: toward a participatory approach. *Philosophical Psychology*, May 24, 2025, pp. 1–27.

Vickers, Clayton, "20 percent say violence may be needed to get the US back on track: Poll," *The Hill*, April 3, 2024.

Wallis, Beth," Oklahoma schools resist the order to teach from the Bible in classrooms," *NPR,* September 12, 2024.

Wang, Zhechen, et. al. "A world together: Global citizen identification as a basis for prosociality in the face of COVID-19," *Sage Journals.* 2023 Vol 26, Issue 1.

Whitman, Walt. *Leaves of Grass: The Original 1855 Edition.* American Renaissance Books, 2009.

Wigglesworth, Cindy. *SQ21: The Twenty-One Skills of Spiritual Intelligence*, Select Books, 2014.

Wilber, Ken. *A Brief History of Everything.* Shambhala, 2007.

Wolpe, Rabbi David J.. *Floating Takes Faith: Ancient Wisdom for a Modern World,* Behrman House, 2004.

Yu, Mallory, "Extremely American' explores the Christian theocracy movement in the U.S," *NPR: All Things Considered,* Aug 31, 2024.

Films

Adra, Basel and Yuval Abraham, directors. *No Other Land.* 2024.

Axelman, Erin&Sam Eilerston, directors. *Israelism*. 2023.

Caro, Niki, director. *Whale Rider. 2002*

Capra, Frank, director. *Mr. Deeds Goes to Town.* 1936.

Davidson, Eron and Ana Nogueira, directors. *Roadmap to Apartheid.* 2012.

Gerwig, Greta, director. *Barbie.* Warner Bros. 2023.

Herman, Marc, director. *The Boy in the Striped Pajamas.* 2008.

Jewison, Norman, director. *Fiddler on the Roof.* 1971.

Lee, Ang, director. *Life of Pi.* 2012.

Websites

A Land for All: Two States. One Homeland. https://www.2s1h.org/en

Christians United for Israel (CUFI). *Press Releases.* December 22, 2020. https://cufi.org/press-releases/cufi-reaches-10-million-members/

Face-to-Face: A Jewish-Palestinian Reparations Alliance. *Kehilla Community Synagogue.*https://kehillasynagogue.org/act/face-to-face-a-jewish-palestinian-reparations-alliance/

Institute for the Advancement of Philosophy for Children, Montclair State University, New Jersey https://www.montclair.edu/iapc/

Interfaith America. https://www.interfaithamerica.org/

Interfaith Leadership Council of Metro Detroit. "Religious Diversity Journeys" https://detroitinterfaithcouncil.com/religious-diversity-

Nonviolence International
https://www.nonviolenceinternational.net/

Religion Matters. https://religionmatters.org/

Interfaith Leadership Council of Metro Detroit.
https://detroitinterfaithcouncil.com/religious-diversity-journe

Standing Together. https://www.standing-together.org/en/about-en

Tanenbaum Center for Interreligious Understanding.
https://tanenbaum.org/

World Encounters. https://www.worldreligions.ca/

World Government of World Citizens. https://worldservice.org/

Worldview Journeys. https://worldviewjourneys.com/

Websites of Multifaith Houses

Global House of Friendship & Hope, Assisi, Italy.
https://friendshipandhope.org/

House of One, Berlin, Germany. https://house-of-one.org/en

House of Religions: Dialogue of Cultures, Berne, Switzerland.
https://haus-der-religionen.ch/

Tri-Faith Initiative, Omaha, Nebraska, USA
https://friendshipandhope.org/

Abrahamic Faith House, Abu Dhabi, UAE
https://www.abrahamicfamilyhouse.ae

Lama Foundation, Taos, New Mexico, USA
https://www.lamafoundation.org/

ORIGINAL ART

All the art in this book is original. Sketches of live performances, drawn in the dark of a theater, were then transposed to larger paper. Stamps from my father's collection, including First Day Covers of Israel, were incorporated along with different kinds of paint into each composition.

The paintings were made in the early 2000s and then stored away until an installation was created, along with ceramic pieces, for an exhibit of local Jewish artists commemorating one year after October 7, 2023. I used my art to call the attention of the Jewish community to reclaim Judaism with a new purpose, where integrity and interdependence are more valued than identity and independence. As Ursula K. Le Guin said, *"Sometimes truth goes out of a story and enters a new one."*

Titles of Lauren I. Zinn Originals in order of appearance

The Swimmer (before Dedication)
Next Stop is Gaza, Man (after Foreword)
The Gates - page 1
Munich (Lost Souls) - page 17
The Golf Lesson - page 27
Highway M-115 - page 50
Learn to Swim - page 75
Our Holocaust - page 77
PIP Luminary (digital sculpture) - page 86
Gone, Not Gone - page 98
Unicorn - page 115
Oklahoma (Rabbis) - page 125
Also Together - page 137
Attunement - page 191
Big River (to the Sea) - page 194
L'dor V'dor - page 202
The Magician - page 224

AUTHOR BIO

Lauren Zinn earned her Ph.D. in Educational Planning (UTEP), an interdisciplinary program at The University of Michigan-Ann Arbor, an MA in Philosophy of History at York University, Toronto, MAT Credits in The Advancement of Philosophy for Children at Montclair State University, New Jersey, a Certificate in Gaming-Simulation Design and a BA from The University of Michigan-Ann Arbor.

She is a seminary-ordained interfaith minister, All Faiths Seminary, NYC and completed all coursework for the Modern Rabbi program at Rabbinic Seminary International, NYC, founded by Orthodox Rabbi Joseph H. Gelberman (z'l).

Lauren founded and led *Congregation Jewbilation: Jewish Roots with Interfaith Wings* and the Hebrew Play Group, a spiritually independent Sunday School for Jewish intermarried families. She also taught at the Hebrew School of a conservative synagogue and co-led the children's program at Ann Arbor's Siddha Yoga Center. She has conducted life cycle ceremonies for numerous interfaith couples and families. She has worked in the worlds of corporate and nonprofit training and education.

Lauren's advocacy work includes leading a faith club for Jewish, Muslim, and Christian women post-9/11, coordinating reunification of an Afghan refugee family, participating in Jewish Palestinian Reparations, joining a Jewish and Palestinian Women's dialogue group, engaging in intra-faith dialogue for healing, and serving on the committee for Public Life and Global Community of the Religion Education Association.

This book is to be followed by *Teaching Judaism (or Your Religion) in the Interspiritual Classroom*. Lauren is also the author of a short story for young adults and the illustrator of children's books written by Ruth A. Zinn. Learn more at zinnhouse.com.

ZINNHOUSE LOGO

The figure in the logo contains two ideas:
1) a figure looking down and inward, kneeling to the left, perhaps praying or meditating, exploring an inner universe, and
2) a figure looking up and outward, perhaps dancing or reaching out to the right, exploring the outer universe.
The figure breaks free of confining ideas to evolve.

Designed by chalk artist and cousin, David Zinn.

www.ingramcontent.com/pod-product-compliance
Lightning Source LLC
Chambersburg PA
CBHW070642160426
43194CB00009B/1548